Writer's BLOC III:

Third Biennial Las Vegas Valley Authors' Showcase

Henderson Writers' Group
&
Mystic Publishers
Henderson, Nevada
2010

Copyright 2010
By
Henderson Writers' Group
(www.hendersonwritersgroup.com/866-869-7842)
Printed in the United States of America
All rights reserved.
ISBN: 978-1-934051-49-8

The material in Writer's Bloc III: the Third Biennial Las Vegas Valley Authors' Showcase, represents the artistic visions of the authors published herein and is their sole property, all rights reverting to the authors upon publication. No part of this collection may be reproduced, stored in a retrieval system, or transmitted by any means—electronic, mechanical, photocopying, recording, or otherwise—without written permission of the individual authors. The authors may be contacted through the HWG website, www.hendersonwritersgroup.com or through Mystic Publishers at 866-869-7842.

Mystic Publishers
614 Mosswood Dr.
Henderson, NV 89002
www.mysticpublishers.com

The stories contained on the pages of this book are dedicated to all those writers who aspire toward publication and all those published authors who's work brought us into the craft.

From the President

As president and founder of the Henderson Writers' Group it is my privilege every other year to introduce our anthology. In this, our third authors' collection, the talented writers of our group have brought you some incredible stories.

In the ten years of our existence, this group continues to grow in their dedication to the written word. Our creative minds will always strive to take our readers from the depths of a murderer's mind to the farthest reaches of outer space. We desire to touch readers of all ages who seek knowledge or entertainment. We revel in the opportunity to share our work and our knowledge. When we are lucky enough to publish our work and pick up readers along the way, we are the ones who grow.

This year's collection will deliver even more diversity than our previous offerings. I hope you enjoy the following pages. If you would like to send us your comments, feel free to do so. Any author in this book can be contacted through the group website:

www.hendersonwritersgroup.com

Thank you for your patronage and—
no matter what book you hold in your hand—

"Enjoy the Read"

Jo A. Wilkins
HWG Founder/President

Judges Comment

It was both an honor and a privilege for me and my colleagues to have been asked to choose the stories and poems contained in this anthology. We were astounded by the abundance of originality and creativity that these writers possessed, it was truly difficult to choose just a few! It is always a blessing when one is presented with the opportunity to enjoy a task and this was truly one of those opportunities.

We are all avid readers and shared a sincere respect and admiration for the talented writers in this group. We found these stories and poems reflective of individuals who demonstrate a passion for the art of writing and storytelling. The poems evoked emotion in us and often painted beautiful pictures with words. The fiction, nonfiction, and short stories kept us in suspense, made us laugh, touched our hearts and encouraged our imaginations to wander. We respect the courage it takes for an artist to offer up his or her work for judgment.

Writers often share their souls with readers and that was certainly the case with these poems and stories. At times, it was difficult to remember that we were to critique the work, as the stories and poems were so engaging that we preferred to read for the sheer enjoyment of reading. I have judged many writing contests and this one had a remarkable variety of writing styles. The Henderson Writers Group is truly a talented group of artists!

This was a wonderful experience and we hope to be involved in next year's project. Our sincere thanks go out to the authors for allowing us to join them on this fantastic journey of creativity and imagination. We hope that you will continue to work on your craft and will further develop the skills and talent that you have demonstrated so aptly in this body of work. We wish you all continued success in your writing careers.

Best regards,
Tracy L. McMurry

....

The HWG would like to express our thanks to the judges from National University who worked so diligently on evaluating our stories. They made the process of choosing between our members submissions easier than in previous years. The judges who worked on this selection are:

Tracy L. McMurry
Associate Regional Dean

Karen Hannington
Admissions Advisor and Published Author

Caprice Houston-Bey
Lead Faculty - School of Education

Contents

POETRY

Real	~ 1 ~	John Dohanich
I Never Told My . . .	~ 2 ~	Kathie Harrington
My sister	~ 3 ~	Leslie Hoffman
I am the Space Between . . .	~ 4 ~	
Light...And Dark	~ 6 ~	Roger Storkamp

STORIES

Grandma's Rattler	~ 11 ~	Grace Andrews
Murder at Hadbury Manor	~ 17 ~	Alba Arango
Me, My Dad and Josh	~ 33 ~	Paul Atreides
Extra $$$	~ 45 ~	Darlien C. Breeze
Throwaways	~ 51 ~	Garry Buzick
The Selection	~ 61 ~	A. L. Campbell
The Love That Transcends	~ 69 ~	Alejandro E. Czeisler
The Dyatlov Incidnet	~ 77 ~	Douglas A. Davy
Flamingo Wash	~ 91 ~	Carol Deanna
A Mini Love Story	~ 105 ~	Sid Goodman
Petty Theft	~ 113 ~	Carrie Ann Lahain
Interview With Lodi	~ 125 ~	Lynn Lanier
Unhappy Friday	~ 137 ~	Linda Lou
The Yesterday Before	~ 141 ~	Michael Molony
Silent Night, Holy War	~ 149 ~	Kevin Parsons
Seductive	~ 161 ~	Debie Prince
Those Oldies But Goodies	~ 165 ~	Donald Riggio
Jenny and the Model T Ford	~ 175 ~	Nancy Sansone
Justice is Served	~ 181 ~	Glory Wade
My Life as a Sperm	~ 185 ~	W. Darrah Whitaker
First Encounter	~ 195 ~	J.A. Wilkins
Emily's Big Day	~ 209 ~	Brian Yates

YOUTH CONTEST WINNER

31 Days	~ 217 ~	Ariel Belanger

CONTRIBUTORS

~ 225 ~

Writer's BLOC III

Poetry

Real
J M Dohanich

It's not real
I only dreamed it
Is there no safe place
No matter, where I cower

I only dreamed it
Still absolute fun
No matter… where I cower
New place new time

Still absolute fun
Is there no safe place
New place… new time
It's not real

I Never Told My Son He Couldn't Dance
Kathie Harrington

I never told my son he couldn't dance.
I never thought he didn't have a chance.

I never told my son he might not read.
I only sought to plant the seed.

I never showed my son a star
That, I felt, was way too far.

I never taught my son to fly,
But I gave him wings on which to try.

I never questioned God's intent.
I only hoped my time well spent.

We never know what life will bring.
I only know that I must sing.

I never told my son he couldn't dance.
That is why he had a chance.

My son, Doug, is today, 38 years old. He has autism. Doug graduated from Chaparral High School, Las Vegas, Nevada, with a class rank of 72 out of 474. He attended UNLV and was a drummer with the Star of Nevada Marching Band. Doug is gainfully employed at a premiere resort on the Las Vegas Strip where he works in a world-class spa. He drives a car, is happy, fulfilled, and contributes to the smiles of those who surround him. Doug is a taxpayer and dances everyday!

My Sister
Leslie Hoffman

Not so long ago
I found you in the Poet & Patriot
drinking Guinness, laughing
under a poster of Che.
I fell in love that day
with your Che
and you
my free spirit sister
the activist
ghost dancer
catcher of dreams
seeker of illusions.

Today
I find you on a bench
in the garden at Villa Soquel
gazing out to sea
ferals rubbing against your ankles.
I sit by you
you smile into infinity.
confined, they say, for your safety
yet, still my free spirit sister
dancing with resident ghosts
weaving dreams
dwelling in illusion.

I am the Space Between an Upturned Rock and the Earth...
Michael O'Neal

I am the space between an upturned rock and the earth
Scattering insects and worms
A retreating shadow wiped away by the sun
Or engulfed by the night
A reluctant void where something seems to be
Invisible without touch
Without a reason nor a cause
Or a meaning
Blown away and filled with wind
But without direction nor flow
Static yet hungry
With a want that warms like mist
With the weight of fog smothering fields of stone.

I sometimes am the stone, hard and unyielding
Save by the mallet and spike
Silent in the beating of the soil
Pressing its weight in vain
To crush the cities of worms and pillbugs
To snap the backs of the centipede trollies
To stop the world
While the world above, where he is only a stone
Weathers him away
In small cycles, to dust and dirt
Feeding those in time of the generations he tries to kill
Until the boot rests on his face
And the hammer hits his brow.

I wish to be the dirt, an infinite memory
A home to worms and nations
A home to rock and roots
Layers of what once we were
A history in sediment, neither space nor stone
Yet changing and somewhat fluid
As a river of mud choking the old
But replanting the new
Neither god nor devil
Alive and dead
Stagnant but growing
Like a redwood towering to at last brush the blue
With but one of its leaves.

Light . . . And Dark
Roger Storkamp

A morning yawn, Sun's outstretched arm
Embraces quaint shops, cobblers, carvers, and the like
Pierces the broken glass, to Guiseppi's bench.
A jangle of strings, dangling arms, legs
Amid dreams of becoming a real boy.

Tiny dust doves made visible in the beam,
Settle on the sleeping stubbled face
Creased and etched with lonely years.
The carver, dreams of wooden people
Content to be the wooden people his scalpel had intended.

Yet within the scrapes, on the wood envisions,
the carving tool its own way does make
the face beyond that which he had intended.
A wish he'd not admit he carves into the toy
Please make me a real life boy.

Not within his dreams nor on his shelf
do we find the carver's secret self.
But through the lies his puppet tells
does the appendage of his desire grow.

The lie that lies within his heart
As shown in his puppet's nose
Lies the phallus of his dreams.
To wake to find the real life boy.

Thus, do we learn the bent of his desires.
The empty shell an old man's breast
Bereft of love and gentle female touch
content to fondle wooden toy.
God, give that man no real boy

Stories

Grandma's Rattler
Grace Andrews

At first light, Grandpa, Dad, and Uncle Jack left the Bowser Mine to work another claim near Pearasol Peak in Southern Oregon. They always left plenty of guns for the women's protection. After all, we were living in the territory of wild animals. Once in a while, the men would come home with a deer, rabbit, quail, pheasant, or even a rattlesnake to eat. Grandma, Mom, and Aunt Shirley all refused to cook snake, let alone eat it, and made sure its carcass was buried deep in the forest.

When I was seven-years-old, our camp was a hundred times better than the year before when we had to share the large tent. The men had built two cabins and a cookhouse in early spring. Aunt Shirley, Uncle Jack, and their new baby were in one cabin. Mom, Dad, and I were in the other cabin. Grandma and Grandpa slept in the modern cookhouse—it had running water and a real toilet. We had to use empty coffee cans during the night. Grandma and Grandpa could use the real thing.

Tailings from the gold mine provided good gravel for the large flat parking area that was used for pickups, dump trucks, and other equipment. The lot separated the two cabins from the cookhouse. Grandpa's gold mine was on the

Writer's Bloc III

upper side of the lot where its dark path went into the guts of the mountain.

To make life easier, Dad and Grandpa ran a galvanized pipe deep inside the tunnel - much further than I wanted to explore—for water. Liquid rained from inside the timbered ceiling of the mine. The open end of the pipe lay on top of the small railroad tracks that supported the ore cart in and out of the mine. All our meat was kept in several large crock pots, with lids, deep inside the tunnel where it was dark, cold, and wet. My job every day was to retrieve meat for dinner. I had to walk very soft on the iron tracks and not on the supporting wood planks. It was real easy to stir up the muddy ground. That dirt would always find its way to the open end of the water pipe. Gravity moved the precious fluid out of the mine and down to the cookhouse. Once outside, the water followed the pipe's course along the edge of the parking area and across the beginning of the steep path that worked its way into the cookhouse sink and faucet. As the pipe got closer to the cookhouse, it followed the downward grade. Air wanting to escape sang the loudest right next to the path.

Lost in my dream world, I walked down the path, careful to step over the water pipe, and on down to the cookhouse for lunch. The pipe rattled—so I thought. Not afraid, I took a few more steps before I froze with one foot still in the air as the sound of a baby's rattle shook again. This time, it was on my left! I stopped, looked at the pipe on my right, and waited for it to shake again. But, it didn't. The clamoring noise was still on my left, in the forbidden playground of thick brush and poison oak that loved to attack me with its blistery rash. There, it sounded again. A cold stiff wave pushed my arm hairs straight up. This time, I knew what it was…a rattlesnake. As brave as possible, I made my way to the cookhouse, ever so careful to place each foot in front of the other and in the middle of the dirt path. Boy, I didn't want to be anywhere near that danger.

When I walked into the cookhouse, Mom was ironing one of my dresses on the towel covered table with one of the two hot irons. Their heavy mass was heated by the hot wood stove. Using a hot pad to hold onto the metal handle, she would use one iron till it cooled, then exchange it for a hot one and continue her job.

Grandma sat next to the window. Her crochet hook moved with the motion of the rocking chair. The sunlight brightened each stitch as her nimble bony fingers moved the tiny hook that barely caught the hair-thin thread. Even in the woods, Grandma was dressed as if she was ready to shop at the five and dime. Her dark hair, cut in the fashion and color of the day, was perfectly combed. At mid-calf, the hemline of a crisp clean dress covered her rolled-up hosiery, the kind that a rubber band held up just below her knees. Long slender feet didn't look wide enough to support her thin body. Grandma looked like she would break in half if anyone squeezed her too hard.

"There's a rattlesnake out there," I said.

Everyone turned toward me with a "yeah, right" look.

"It's just the pipe," Grandma said, not losing the rhythm of a stitch.

"Uhuh, there's a snake out there," pointing to the cabin wall safely between us and danger. No one believed me. Frustrated, I went back outside to make sure I was right. Dad had impressed upon me how air in the water pipe sounded just like a rattlesnake's tail. I concentrated on that sound just in case I did not hear the real thing. Yep, the noise still came from the wrong side of the path. I marched right back inside with more determination.

"There is a rattlesnake out there!" I said in a stronger voice.

Grandma put her doily down. "Okay, show me where it is. It's probably one of the wild cats doing his job out there.

Tom always catches mice around here."

Outside, I took her to a safe place to stand in the path. We stood there until she heard it, too.

"Come back inside with me," she whispered. "You get the gun and shells while I put something else on." Back inside the cookhouse, she slipped on a pair of Grandpa's jeans, cinching the waist tight under her dress, took her shoes off, and laced on a pair of his high work boots.

It didn't matter what kind of gun it was, even I knew how to shoot a snake. The only thing necessary was the nerve to hold the gun steady while the snake lined its head up with the barrel, ready to attack. One slow squeeze of the trigger would blow its head off.

I grabbed her Colt .38 and found the box for its shells. It looked like it was made special to just snuggle in the palm of her hand. "Grandma, the box is empty."

"Look again. There has to be something," she said.

I showed her the empty box, "See, there's nothing. Only shotgun shells."

Remembering that the men had used her gun for target practice, she realized they did not replace the bullets and said, "Okay, hand me that shotgun and shells." Her nimble fingers shoved the shells into each barrel and clicked the gun into ready mode. "Damn it, the firing pin is stuck! It's too dangerous to use." Of course, there was no ammo for the Luger that Dad brought home from the war. The men had all the working guns; the women had nothing that worked. The guys figured we were safe in camp. Ha!

We went to the rear of the cabin and entered the attached tent-bathroom. Grandpa had put in a toilet at the rear of the tent. Next to it, he installed a turn handle to control the flow of water at its bottom to flush the waste from the toilet bowl into a gutter, out the tent, and down the hillside. No need to dig a hole for any outhouses now. Besides the 'poddy' room, the tent was used to store canned food and tools for the mine and campsite.

Grandma grabbed a shovel with a flat head and led me through the tent flap outside.

"Stay put," she told me and headed into the bush. Afraid to move, I stood like a statue on the gravel path. I could hear where she was by the moving noise caused by walking on dead leaves, twigs, and brushing her body against the thick maze. It did not take her long to start making a lot of racket. I tried to imagine what was going on, but had no idea. It was like she was shaking all the leaves and branches off the manzanita, poison oak, and scrub brush. Then, silence. I strained to hear any sound. My eyes stared hard to see into the dense foliage, but I could not see Grandma anywhere. I got scared for her. Then, I heard a little bit of noise, and then the noise moved. I watched with my ears and followed the sound to where Grandma first entered the brush.

Curious, but still frozen, I watched her come closer and closer to me. The head of the shovel was parallel with the ground. On it, a big fat snake. Its long body filled the shovel. A piece of skin held the head as it dangled off the front of the flat metal. There were ten good rattles on the tail. This was a snake that had been around for a long time. I didn't like my first close-up experience with it. I did not want to touch the scary thing and jumped when the tail slipped off the shovel with Grandma's movement. Keeping the bulk of the snake on the shovel, she placed it over a mass of fallen leaves.

"Look how it blends into other colors." Then, she moved the shovel onto the gravel and the snake changed again. I couldn't believe it. That snake was dead, but its skin was still alive.

"This is why you have to be careful; they can change to blend into their surroundings."

"Why was the snake mad?" I asked.

"Tom cornered the snake and lay ready to pounce on it.

At the same time, the snake sat coiled up ready to spring onto Tom. I got there just as they were set to strike each other. You stay near the cabin," Grandma told me. "I'm going to bury this so the men don't find it. They'll want to eat it, and I'm not going to have any snake in my cookhouse."

She carried her trophy down the hill, way behind the tent, and buried it.

When Grandma returned, she explained, "I cut the head all the way off and buried it real deep. That way, the wild animals cannot eat the head and the poison inside it."

"Why?"

"Honey, the way spiders and bugs like to nibble you, I didn't want to take the chance of them gnawing the snake's head, then carrying the venom inside their body, and maybe one of them biting you. You know how allergic you are to bug bites. It would be more dangerous if you were bit by something that ate poison from the snake's head."

From then on, Grandma made sure she had a working gun within her reach when the men were away from camp.

Murder at Hadbury Manor
Alba Arango

I glanced at the Medic team anxiously holding their equipment. At 6:30 this morning, the Chief called saying Milton Hadbury had been murdered during the night. His crazy mansion had a time lock attached to every door and window, making it impossible for anyone to enter or exit the house from 7:00 p.m. to 7:00 a.m.

At 7:00 a.m. exactly, the iron door flew open.

"Where's the body?" the coroner asked the six frantic faces who greeted us.

Everyone pointed to a room in the center of the house. Man, did they look freaked-out.

"My name is Detective Joe Simmons," I said calmly. "Let's find someplace a bit more comfortable, and you can all tell me exactly what happened."

"The library's over there," a short heavyset man pointed. I eyed him carefully. The balding man was in his late forties and dressed in a three-piece suit.

"Thank you, Mr...?"

"Green," the man replied. "Thomas Green."

"Mr. Green," I acknowledged. "Why don't you lead the way?"

The man grunted but complied. I plopped on the library

sofa and pulled out a small notebook and my old blue pen.

I turned to the three men and three women in the room. "Let's start at the beginning."

An older, gentle-looking woman with graying hair cleared her throat. "My name is Lydia Peacock. I'm Milton's neighbor."

"All right, Mrs. Peacock." I scribbled in my notebook. "What happened?"

Her voice was shaky. "We all received invitations from Milton to play one of those murder-mystery games."

"Milt was crazy about games," the beautiful Asian woman interrupted.

"And you are...?"

"Scarlet," she answered in a sultry voice, that well suited her exotic appearance. "Samantha Scarlet." Her red velvet gown had a slit up to mid-thigh. She lit a long slender cigarette.

I tore my eyes away from her. "You were all invited to participate in a party game?"

"That's right," a gruff-looking older man confirmed. "We showed up around 4:00. Milton took us to our rooms and told us to look around. Dinner was at 6:00, and he'd see us then. He seemed in unusually good spirits."

"Unusually good spirits," I repeated, watching the white-haired man carefully. "I didn't get your name."

"Colonel Samuel Mustard. Hadbury's my brother."

"Why would you say Mr. Hadbury was in unusually good spirits? Was that uncommon?"

"Ha!"

The interjection came from a small, elderly woman with silver hair. "That man was never in good spirits."

"Your name, Ma'am?"

"Muriel White. I was Milton Hadbury's housekeeper for thirty years, and I'll be the first to tell you, that man never smiled."

"Not around you," Miss Scarlet purred.

"Don't talk like that to me, you little harlot!"

"Now, now," I said calmly. Emotions seemed to be escalating. "Let's get back to the evening. You were escorted to your rooms and told to look around. Then, what happened?"

"Hadbury disappeared," a brown-haired man in his mid-thirties replied. He wore a brown sports coat and gold wire-rimmed glasses. Total nerd.

"Disappeared?" I scrawled. "You didn't see him again, Mr...?"

"Professor Randolph Plum," the man answered. "And, no, none of us did, until dinner."

"What happened at dinner?"

"Nothing really," Mr. Green said. "Hadbury just served dinner and said he'd explain the rules of the game afterward."

Something in Mr. Green's statement caught my attention.

"Mr. Hadbury served you dinner himself?" I asked curiously. "Surely, a man of Hadbury's wealth has servants to do his work."

"He does," Mrs. Peacock's timid voice explained. "But, Milton gave them the weekend off."

If no servants were in the house, and if the doors and windows were time-locked at 7:00 p.m., then one of these six people must be the killer.

"Detective!" a voice called me from outside the room.

I smiled at the suspects. "Excuse me a moment."

I walked to the conservatory in the center of the house. Sunlight from the skylights illuminated the room. Hadbury's body lay on its back.

"Do we know what killed him?" I asked the policeman kneeling over the body.

"It looks like severe blows to the back of the head with a blunt object. And, take a look at this." He pointed to the floor.

Writer's Bloc III

"Looks like he was dragged here."

Hadbury wasn't murdered in the greenhouse? Very interesting.

"I apologize for that interruption," I said, back in the library. "Where were we? Ah, yes. Dinner. What happened after dinner?"

"We moved into the ballroom," Mr. Green took up the story. "Hadbury handed us each an envelope for that crazy game of his. There was a huge clap of thunder and the lights went out."

"He lit some candles," Mrs. White said, "but the lights never came back on."

"Finally, at about 8:00," Colonel Mustard continued, "he said to forget it. We couldn't play the game in the dark, so he told us to go to our rooms and we'd play in the morning."

"Was that the last time you saw him?"

The Colonel nodded.

I looked at each suspect. "Who found him?"

"I did," Mrs. Peacock said softly. "I came downstairs at 5:30 to have some coffee and noticed the light on in the greenhouse. I walked in and saw Milton on the floor. He wasn't breathing." Her voice became shaky. "I didn't know what to do so I... I...," her voice trailed off.

"Screamed," Professor Plum finished. "Loudly."

"I heard the scream," Miss Scarlet said, "and believed it was part of the game. I got out of bed and fixed myself up."

"I thought the same as Miss Scarlet," Mr. Green added. "That's why I'm wearing this stuffy suit."

"I think that's true for us all," Mrs. White said. "None of us knew what had really happened."

"One of us did," Miss Scarlet murmured.

"What do you mean?" Mrs. Peacock asked.

"One of us had to be the killer."

Uneasiness came over the group. I closed my notebook

and stood up. "You should all go back to your rooms. I'll need to speak with you individually, and you may enjoy changing into more comfortable clothes."

The six suspects walked up the stairs. The killer couldn't have killed Hadbury and dragged his body downstairs without someone noticing. The murder must have taken place downstairs.

I decided to examine each room for myself, starting with the kitchen. Plates were piled high next to the sink. Nothing unusual.

Next came the study. I scanned the room carefully. Something under the wine-colored sofa was sticking out. I walked over and pulled out a long strand of rope tied into a noose. Strange. Very strange.

The great hall, draped with ornate tapestries, led me to the lounge. A beautiful black piano decorated one corner. I sat on an Elizabethan-style chair and looked around.

One of the curtains was ruffled. I walked over to straighten it and something fell. A small lead pipe. It could be the murder weapon. But, why would the killer have been so clumsy about hiding it? Weird.

Next came the library. Thousands of books gleamed from the endless bookshelves. A beautiful Bombay trunk caught my eye. I opened it, and…surprise! Inside lay a large metal wrench. A rope, a lead pipe, and a wrench. What the heck was going on?

I walked into the next room and fell in love. The main feature was a beautiful hand-carved mahogany billiard table. The contemporary furniture gave this room a modern edge, different than the others.

I sat on a barstool and spun around. Noticing a large brass candlestick looking incredibly out of place in the ultra-modern room, I picked it up and turned it over in my hands. Very heavy. Yet another potential weapon.

The dining room proved fruitless, so I moved into the

Writer's Bloc III

ballroom. This was the last room where anyone had seen Hadbury alive.

Tables and chairs outlined the room and a small stage with a podium graced the end of the ballroom. I casually opened the podium drawer. A revolver.

Then, I had an epiphany.

"Stupid!" I scolded myself. Of course, there were weapons all around the house. Hadbury had invited everyone there for a murder party game. The weapons were just props. I grabbed the revolver and opened it. No bullets.

Enough. Time for the interviews. I climbed the stairs, brooding over not figuring out the secret of the weapons earlier.

There were six bedrooms in this wing of the mansion. I knocked on the first door near the staircase. Mr. Green answered.

"May I come in?"

The heavyset man grunted and waved me in. The room was lavishly decorated with flowered carpet, brass candlesticks, and a huge brass chandelier.

"I need to ask you some questions about last night." I opened my notebook. "What time did you settle in for the night?"

"Right after Hadbury dismissed us, about 8:00."

"Did you notice anything strange during the night?"

"I was asleep most of the time. I did hear the professor's door open for a few minutes."

"What time was that?" I asked, scribbling in my notebook.

"I don't know, exactly. Maybe twelve or twelve-thirty."

"Anything else?"

"You're wasting your time with these questions. I can tell you who the killer is."

"Really?" I asked. "Who?"

"Miss Scarlet."

"What makes you say that?"

"She's been mad at Hadbury for not divorcing that estranged wife of his." Mr. Green's voice dropped to a whisper. "Rumor has it he just added Scarlet to his will. Ten-to-one she killed him before he changed his mind."

I left the room, closing the door behind me. Money is a very good motive. Professor Plum answered the next door.

"Come in, Detective."

The décor of the room was the same as Mr. Green's. I walked carefully across the room. Notepaper was scattered everywhere.

"Working on a project?"

"Always," the professor said with a laugh.

I flipped the page of my notebook. "What time did you get to your room last night?"

"Probably around 9:00 or so."

"What did you do from 8:00 until 9:00?"

"I browsed through the library. Hadbury has some unusual books, and I was hoping to find something to help with my research."

"Wasn't that kind of hard to do with the power out?"

"Not when you have a penlight." Professor Plum pulled a blue penlight from his pocket. It produced a fairly extensive light.

"Did you notice anything unusual last night?"

"Only doors opening and closing all night long."

"Doors opening and closing?" I repeated.

The professor nodded. "First, Mr. Green's door opened around 9:45. Then, the Colonel's door opened at 11:00 and again at 12:30. Then Mr. Green's door opened again at 5:00. It was ridiculous."

"Did you go anywhere last night or open your door for anything?"

"No. I was in my room working all night long." The professor began fumbling through his notes, nervously.

"By candlelight or flashlight?"

"Flashlight. Until the electricity came back."

I stopped scribbling. "When was that?"

"Around 12:15."

"Do you know anyone who might have wanted to kill Hadbury?"

Professor Plum finished rummaging through his papers. "It was Mr. Green, without a doubt."

"Why Mr. Green?"

"Green is Hadbury's son-in-law. Last month, he asked Hadbury to pay for his son's college tuition. He refused, and they had a huge fight."

"You think Mr. Green killed Hadbury out of anger?"

"Not anger. Money. If Hadbury died, his inheritance would easily cover the tuition."

"Thank you, Professor."

I left, gazing blankly into the empty hallway. Now, there were two possible suspects with monetary motives. But why did the professor lie about opening his door?

Next.

"Sorry to bother you, Colonel, but I need to ask you some questions."

He motioned for me to enter, and I noticed a monocle hanging from the pocket of his shirt. Who uses a monocle anymore?

"Colonel, what time did you get back to your room last night?"

"About 8:15." He lit a stunning antique pipe.

"Were you in your room all night?"

"Yes. Except for a quick trip to the kitchen for some water."

"What time was that?"

"Around 11:00 or so. I passed Mrs. White in the hall. She had the same idea I did."

The first to admit he left his room.

"Had the electricity returned by then?"

"No. I had to use a candle."

"Did you notice anything unusual during the night?"

"I did hear a door open at about 5:00 this morning. It was too far away to be Plum's. It was probably Green's."

"Do you have any idea who would want Hadbury dead?"

The Colonel took a long drag on his pipe. "I don't like to point fingers, but I have heard her threaten him before."

"Who?"

"Mrs. Peacock. She and Hadbury argued for years over the border between their properties. Last year, Hadbury took her to court and won. She swore she'd get even."

"You think Mrs. Peacock killed him for revenge?"

That sweet old woman? Really?

"Revenge, and the fact that Hadbury left her the property in his will."

"Thank you, Colonel." I reached for the door.

Now, there were three distinct motives. Perhaps, the women could shed some light on things.

I knocked on the first door across the hall. Mrs. White answered.

"Hello, Detective. Are you still trying to figure out who killed Hadbury?"

I walked into the room. "Let's just say I'm trying to piece together exactly what happened last night."

"Don't waste your time. I'll tell you who did it."

"Pray tell," I encouraged. This should be good.

"It's Hadbury's lousy brother, the Colonel."

"Colonel Mustard?"

"You sound surprised," Mrs. White noticed.

"With that lashing you gave Miss Scarlet earlier, I thought she'd be your first suspect."

"She's no good, mind you. But, I don't think she's a killer. The Colonel, though, he's as bad as they come."

"Why would Colonel Mustard want to kill his brother?"

Writer's Bloc III

"This house and the whole manor belonged to their parents. If Hadbury were to die, Samuel would get it all."

I flipped the page of my notebook. "Did you notice anything unusual last night? Maybe a door opening or strange sounds?"

"Not really. I did hear the hussy's door open twice, once at midnight and again five minutes later."

"Were you in your room all night?"

"Most of it. I went downstairs for a glass of water."

"In the dark?"

"I had a flashlight," she pulled out her keys and displayed a flashlight keychain.

"Did you see anybody else?"

"Only the Colonel. He was leaving his room just as I was coming back...probably on his way to kill poor Hadbury."

"Thank you, Mrs. White."

I shut the door and bit my lip. Four motives?

Miss Scarlet opened the door, wearing a revealing halter top and skin tight jeans. "Hello again, Detective," she said and sauntered across the room. She half-laid on the bed and smiled seductively. "Is it my turn to be examined?"

I decided to stay near the safety of the door. "I just need to ask you a few questions."

"Anything," she said softly.

I cleared my throat. "What time did you come to your room last night?

She sat up on the bed. "Around 9:00. I tried to get Milt to have a nightcap with me, but he refused. So, I just came back to my room."

"Did you hear or notice anything unusual during the night?"

"I did notice Mrs. White went out for a bit. She left her room at 10:30 and didn't return until 11:00."

"Was that it?"

"Mrs. Peacock's door opened at about 9:45, probably

when she came back to her room. She's an incredibly sound sleeper. I didn't hear a peep from her room until she opened the door at 5:00, and then again at 5:30. Soon after that is when I heard the scream."

I scrawled in my notebook, then looked up at the exotic beauty. "Can you think of anyone who would want Mr. Hadbury dead?"

"Professor Plum. Milt funded his experiments until he found out the good professor had been using the money on genetic alteration. Milt refused to have any part of it and cut his funding completely. The professor was furious."

"You think Professor Plum killed Hadbury out of vengeance?"

She shrugged. "Milt's will does leave a large donation to the university's science department."

"Thanks for your time, Miss Scarlet."

She leaned back on the bed. "Anytime, Detective. Anytime."

One last suspect.

Mrs. Peacock opened the door and timidly invited me in. I smiled. She seemed so sweet.

"Can you tell me what time you returned to your room last night?"

"Just after Hadbury said goodnight, around 8:00."

"Did you notice anything unusual during the night? Strange sounds, doors, anything?"

"I did hear Mrs. White out in the hallway. I think she was talking to one of the gentlemen."

"What time was that?"

"Around 11:00."

"Did you leave your room at all last night?"

"No." She fumbled with the lace on her dress. "I was in my room all night."

"Do you know of anyone who would want to kill Hadbury?"

"Well," she lowered her eyes. "I can't say for sure."

"Mrs. Peacock, if you know anything, please tell me."

The elderly lady sighed. "I don't like to make accusations, but I do know Mrs. White has been struggling ever since she retired. My housekeeper says Mrs. White complains constantly about how Hadbury's pension isn't enough to live on."

"You think Mrs. White killed Hadbury for retribution?"

"Not exactly. Mrs. White is in Hadbury's will. He made sure she would be taken care of after he died."

"I see." I kept my eyes on the woman.

"Please, Detective," Mrs. Peacock seemed distressed. "I don't want to accuse her. She's a nice lady. I just can't believe anybody would..." Her voice trailed off into sobs.

I touched her arm sympathetically. "It'll be okay. We'll find whoever did this."

I headed downstairs. Too many things didn't add up. I entered the billiard room, sat on a bar stool, and took out my notebook.

All six guests were in his will. All six had a motive.

I rubbed my eyes. The answer was right in front of me...somewhere on those sheets of paper. My eyes fixed on the brass candlestick. I thought of all the weapons hidden around the house by Hadbury.

Suddenly, it hit me. I looked down at my notes. "I've got it!"

I waved a policeman over. "Round up the suspects and bring them here."

They walked in nervously, and I motioned for them to be seated.

"First off, I want to thank you all for putting up with my questions."

"Can we go now?" Mr. Green asked gruffly.

"Not quite yet," I answered slowly. "You see, each person in this room is guilty of either lying or keeping information from me. But, only one of you murdered Hadbury."

"You know who did it?" Miss Scarlet asked, her eyes flashed.

"Yes, but first, I think you all deserve to know what really happened at Hadbury Manor last night."

Six pairs of eyes stared at me intently.

"We'll start with you, Miss Scarlet." I walked around to face her.

"Me?" Miss Scarlet said, surprised.

"Your actions last night are easily accounted for. Hadbury dismissed the group at 8:00, but you hung around attempting to woo his affection. When he turned you down, you went to your room around 9:00."

I started pacing.

"Not wanting to waste an entire evening, you decided to prey on the only single, younger man in the house, Professor Plum. You knocked on his door at midnight and attempted to seduce him. After a few minutes of discussion, he declined, and you returned to your room at 12:05, where you remained until you heard the scream."

"You little hussy," Mrs. White seethed. "Betraying the master in his own house. And, with a complete stranger!"

"Don't get so worked up, housekeeper." Miss Scarlet smiled. "Who do you think convinced Milt to fund the professor's work to begin with?"

Professor Plum turned slightly red. "That was a long time ago. I assure you, nothing happened last night."

"I know," I said. "I believe Professor Plum was indeed working in his room all night. Neither he nor Miss Scarlet is the killer."

"So, who did it?" Mr. Green demanded.

"Mr. Green." I turned to face him. "You were actually a prime suspect. You claimed to be in your room at 8:00, but someone heard your door open at 9:45. At first, I thought you were lying to me, until I realized, it didn't have to be you who opened the door."

"If he didn't open the door, then who did?" Miss Scarlet asked.

"Would you like to answer that Mrs. Peacock, or shall I?"

Mrs. Peacock turned pale and looked like she was about to faint. I walked over and touched her shoulder reassuringly.

"The reason you didn't hear a sound from Mrs. Peacock's room all night," I explained to Miss Scarlet, "is because she wasn't in her room all night. She left her room at 9:45 and spent the night in Mr. Green's room. Then at 5:00, she returned to her room, got ready, and went downstairs at 5:30 when she discovered Hadbury's body."

"It's true," Mrs. Peacock said quietly. "We've been having an affair." A tear rolled down her cheek.

"So, you both killed Hadbury," Colonel Mustard accused. "Did he find out and threaten to tell his daughter?"

"We didn't kill him," Mr. Green declared angrily.

"No, you didn't," I confirmed and began pacing around the room again. "Here's how the evening played out for our two remaining suspects. Mrs. White left her room with her flashlight at 10:30 to get a glass of water. At 11:00, she returned to her room."

"A half-hour is enough time to kill someone," Miss Scarlet commented.

"True," I agreed. "But, there's more. The Colonel and Mrs. White passed each other in the hallway at 11:00. That fact was confirmed by pretty much everybody in this room."

I walked over to the bar and pointed to the brass candlestick. "When I first saw this candlestick, I assumed it was one of the weapons Hadbury had placed around the mansion for his crazy mystery game. But, all the other weapons had been hidden."

"What's your point?" Mr. Green asked impatiently.

"The Colonel didn't have a flashlight to light his way, so

he used a candlestick. This candlestick. He walked downstairs and encountered Hadbury in this room. They argued for a while until the Colonel couldn't take it anymore. He picked up his candlestick and beat Hadbury over the head several times, killing him."

Mrs. Peacock began to weep softly.

"The Colonel dragged the body to the conservatory to hide it, then realized there was no way of seeing to get back to the stairway. Taking a chance, he flipped on the switch and was delighted to see the power had returned.

"He left the light on to guide his way back. By morning, the light wouldn't be noticeable with all the sunlight from the skylights. He didn't count on Mrs. Peacock's early morning coffee run."

The Colonel bolted for the door. Two policemen tackled him and slapped on handcuffs.

"He deserved to die!" He screamed as they led him away. "You all know it's true!"

I turned to the remaining group. "You're free to go."

They walked out of the room somberly. Miss Scarlet was the last to leave. She pulled out a card from her back pocket and handed it to me. "If there's ever anything I can do for you, I'd be more than happy to." She smiled seductively, then left. I glanced at the card. It was the name of an Asian massage parlor.

"Simmons," the Chief's voice thankfully interrupted my thoughts.

"Hey, Chief."

"They told me you figured out who killed Hadbury. How'd you do it?"

"Simple. I went to each room, interrogated the suspects, and used the process of elimination."

"And?"

"What can I say? It was Colonel Mustard, in the billiard room, with the candlestick."

Me, My Dad and Josh
Paul Atreides

What a horrendous day. It was already late as my mind focused on the prize: an ice-cold beer, a shower and, above all, naked solitude. With the car carelessly put to bed in the garage and the mail yanked from its nest at the end of the driveway, cardboard legs dragged me into the house. Attempting to separate the junk from the bills, the cranial neurons instantly fired on all eight cylinders at the unmistakable sound of that voice. Sure enough, there he was: sitting on the couch, talking to Josh about college choices.

To put it mildly, I was pissed.

"Well, just don't be stupid. Don't waste your efforts on some ridiculous liberal arts degree. What— " They both turned at the sound of my entrance.

More than a couple seconds passed before my face mustered what might barely pass for a smile. The mail dropped with a thud to the counter, and my lunch bag landed on a shelf in the pantry. While eating lunch out was affordable, now that two households didn't need to be supported, I could not justify spending the money. Frugality: an ingrained lesson from dear ole Dad; probably one of the very few things about me he found commendable.

I crossed into the family room, shook his hand and asked when he'd gotten in, sticking to small pleasantries to keep the conversation as short as possible. More importantly, the inevitable confrontation would be put off. My lousy poker abilities betrayed me; the immediate disappointment on my father's face, and the disapproval on Josh's, made that apparent. His unannounced presence irked me most because he had been dispensing his bullshit advice to my son.

That's my job. My privilege. I'm his father. I earned the right to help him make this decision, not that son-of-a-bitch. Dark memories slammed into my brain. After my father vetoed my choice, it had been a struggle to make my own way through college. And, I still didn't go for the degree I truly desired.

During my senior year in high school, about the same time of year as now, Dad asked, "Have you thought about college yet?"

"Well, yeah! Of course I want to go."

"Where?"

"Kent State University."

We weren't wealthy and, with Kent being so close, the ability to live at home was a bonus, but my choice of schools would have been the same regardless. KSU boasted one of the best theatre programs in the country. Sure, there had been the whole student shooting incident years before; a bunch of high school kids, me included, had even watched the initial march through Kent. It was still my first choice, to major in theatre arts, maybe with a teaching degree, and my argument regarding campus safety was ready.

Doc, my high school drama teacher, had been a big influence on me. He cast me in a small role on my first attempt. After the opening weekend, he stopped me in the hall between classes. "You really handled yourself well up there."

A grin broke out. "Thanks."

"I hope we'll see more of you."

"Absolutely!" The Cheshire Cat smile widened.

Me, My Dad and Josh/Atreides

If giving me a role hadn't landed the fish, that exchange certainly sunk the hook. My parents insisted on after-school work as a requisite to drive any of the family cars, but I kept my hands in the pot three hours each day in the theatre or the music room as a student teacher. At the beginning of senior year, Doc asked if I would audition for the lead role of the fall musical. He was offering me the possibility to play Harold Hill in *The Music Man*? I was so there! Unfortunately, Dad wasn't having any of it. I was not permitted to give up work for something so frivolous as performing arts. Giving up the job meant no money to pay for insurance, and for my father it was simple: No money, no insurance, no driving.

The same mind-set held out for college as well. It wasn't my choice of schools – the idea of theatre bugged him.

"It's a waste," he said, "of your time and my money. I'm not going to put out good money on something as stupid and useless as that."

"No, it's not."

"It *is*. What kind of living can you make with a degree like that?"

"I could teach. Like Doc."

"I won't pay for it."

"But, Dad, why? You promised!"

"My money isn't going to pay for you to learn how to flit around on a stage. Who would pay you to do that?"

"But—"

"Get a business degree, or something reasonable. Otherwise, forget it. Find the money yourself."

"Why? What's wrong with theatre?"

"Not on my dime," he stated as he opened the newspaper in dismissal.

Although he insisted his stance was because theatre would not provide a good living, I thought then and still do, that one word said it all: 'Flit.' It was his narrow-mindedness; the 'queer factor.' Years later, while contemplating school after my discharge from the military, that conversation still haunted me. More than 2,000 miles from home, paying my own way, and his words would not be stifled. That's why engineering became a vocation, a way to pay the bills, slogging through the drudgery each day, forced to satisfy the creative side, my love for the theatre, as an avocation.

Unhappy he had been giving my son college advice, especially when it included his idea of what might be a worthy degree, I excused myself to go change and unwind. I stopped at the fridge, grabbed a beer, and went into the master bedroom slamming the door. The sound echoed through the tiled hallways. I ripped off my work clothes, threw them into a heap on the floor. In staccato bursts of anger, I yanked on a pair of jeans and a T-shirt, and slugged down a good half of the beer. Then, a phone call to Ellen to say I would be on my way in a few minutes.

We had met through our sons, who had become inseparable by the time they were ten years old. Though we hadn't dated for long at this point, perhaps a few months, she already knew how to interpret my moods quickly. She promised she would be waiting with a glass of wine in hand, along with a sympathetic ear.

On the edge of the bed, I glowered in silence, finished my beer and strained to fend off the ghosts and emotions of the past. I threw some clothes into a duffle bag, strode out through the kitchen, and waved without a word. Josh rushed out the door behind me.

"Dad! Why are you so pissed off?"
"Leave it alone, Kiddo."
"No, Dad! Why are you mad?"
"What were you thinking, Josh?"
"What? What is so wrong?"
"Did you invite him, or did he invite himself?"
"Does it matter which way it went?"

"You called and asked him, didn't you? You invited him!"

"So?" Josh stuck his chin in the air, challenging me.

"When were you planning to tell me?" Before he opened his mouth to reply, I said, "That was rhetorical. Obviously, you had no intention of saying anything about it."

"Mom left me her share of the house. It's half mine. I can invite anyone I want!"

Though it was true, my anger hit new levels.

Charlene had left him her entire estate when she died. She had even cut out her long-time, live-in companion; though including the guy wouldn't have changed anything since they died in the same plane crash. So, Josh and I now owned the property in joint tenancy, with custodial control in my name, since he was still a minor.

He wasn't aware we lived in the house, now, only because I had to continue paying the mortgage after the divorce when he was four. That, piled on top of the alimony and child support, made for a decade of monkish existence.

"You're right, Josh: half yours! You could've at least warned me about this visit. But you do what you want," I said waving my hand through the open car window. "Evidently, my opinion doesn't matter, does it?"

I slammed the gearshift into reverse and backed out, leaving him in the garage. I started off down the street, closed the window, cranked the A/C, and then glanced into the rearview mirror. My dad stood at the bottom of the driveway next to a forlorn looking Josh. That may have been a snarky comment to make, especially since he couldn't have known how fast one rancid event with my father could boil over. I slowed and pulled over to the curb, sitting there frustrated and conflicted.

This was not the way we handled things. I taught my son to confront problems head-on, with a calm demeanor. We had always settled things that way. No matter what came up, we faced the trouble together, as rationally as we could muster. And it had never failed us; we'd never reached this point before.

Ever.

I didn't know how to make him understand. Hell, I didn't understand. Knuckles tapped on the glass.

"Sorry, Josh," I started as my head turned toward the sound, but Josh wasn't standing beside the car. A heaving sigh escaped as I pushed the switch to lower the window.

"Sigh all you want. Get over yourself and get your ass back there. Talk to him. You've done a terrific job with this kid. That's my grandson. Don't screw things up."

In renewed seething, my blood pressure rising, I glanced again into the mirror. Josh sat on the curb in front of the house, head hung, motionless. My throat closed up. Tears began to well.

What do you want from me, Kiddo? What do you expect me to do?

I had gotten four houses away from home, a bit more than halfway to the gates at the end of the small cul-de-sac, before pulling to the curb.

"Get in," I managed to say.

"I can walk back."

One fused ankle, two fake knees, and a fake hip, but he could walk. My head shook at his stubbornness. *Well, he walked to me; I guess he could walk back.* I pulled the car around the small median island, parked in the garage, and got out. Josh still sat on the curb.

"Josh." He wouldn't even turn to face me. I stood in the doorway, feeling as defeated as he looked.

As his grandfather approached him, he stood. "Go talk," my father told him.

Josh turned around. I held my hand out to him. He slowly walked toward me but, as he did, an expression crossed his face; the one that always told me he had something up his sleeve. I let him lead the way.

Me, My Dad and Josh/Atreides

The three of us sat on the patio, staring wordlessly at nothing. You would've thought one of us would know how to start. After ten minutes, Josh got up and went into the house. He reappeared with his hands full. In the few minutes he was gone, Dad and I didn't exchange so much as a glance.

"I called Jimmy's mom to tell her you wouldn't be there for a while, 'k?" Josh said as he put a shot glass in front of each of us and a bottle of bourbon at the center of the table.

"What do you think you're doing?" I protested pointing at the bottle.

"Humor me, okay?" He placed an egg timer on the table, set for the maximum. He paused with his hand on it to keep it from starting. "No interruptions. We each get three minutes. No answers, no comments allowed. Just air the problem. Voice the concern. I go first."

He looked at each of us in turn. My father indicated his agreement with the short flick of a hand, I hesitated for a beat and nodded my consent.

"'K, then." He pulled his hand away and the timer started a loud ticking. "I'm tired of this bullshit."

I quickly turned and took a breath to speak. He cut me off. "No, you can't talk. See, it's not your turn. Sorry, I'll try to refrain from the language. The two of you have so much air to clear, how can you breathe? God knows you're suffocating me! You tell me things you won't tell each other. We're all we got, Dad! Don't do this anymore… You gotta help me. I know I should have asked before I told Gramp to come. I knew you'd be pissed; I knew it! That's *why* I didn't ask you. But it's not fair, Dad. It's not. Why can't I see him if I want to? Because of things he did to you and Uncle Tom? Because you harbor grudges? That's bullshit!"

A glare and pointed finger from me issued another warning.

"Sorry. But there's just no other word for it. He's my grandfather, and I love him. I have a right to see him."

He looked to his grandfather as he paused for a moment. With a deep breath, he began again. "And what is it with you? What stops you from admitting you made mistakes, Gramp? Why is it so hard to look Dad or Uncle Tom in the eye and say, 'Sorry son, I fucked up.'"

My hand shot out of its own volition and smacked his arm softly.

"I'm sorry about the language; I'm trying Dad, I *really* am," he insisted. "The two of you act like a couple of school kids. You glower and pout, steam coming out of your ears. But, neither one of you will talk about it. Except to me. To bitch and complain."

He pointed at his grandfather. "Then, you try to pretend nothing happened. Why, Gramp? When something has obviously been upset, why do you always pretend nothing is wrong? I know you think I'm still a kid. I know I've got lots to learn. But I learned already: life's short. I don't have time to waste, not a minute of it. Not on crap like this. That's it." He pushed the egg timer in front of me, "Your turn."

We waited for the ding. Each nerve-wracking tick seemed to take forever, yet the small bell rang too soon for my churning stomach. A good minute passed before I picked the thing up and twisted the dial. After a huge, deep breath, I slowly exhaled and released the timer. Three lousy minutes wouldn't be nearly enough to clear the air. But, maybe it could be a start. I fixed my eyes on my son and realized he was right: life *is* very short. My mouth opened, but unsure of myself, no words came out.

The seconds ticked by, and the knot in my stomach tightened.

Maybe if I don't look at them, I thought and stared out over the back yard after a second failed attempt. It was as if my brain couldn't decide how to begin to squeeze a lifetime of pain into so few words and have them understand. Finally, with a stolen glance at Josh, I dove in.

Me, My Dad and Josh/Atreides

"I'm not angry you invited him, Kiddo." I looked my father in the eye. "And I'm not angry you came." I turned back to Josh. "But you should have asked me first. Not for permission, but because I live here; I pay the bills."

Realizing a remark like that sounded just like my dad, a short huff of breath escaped my throat. I shook my head and gazed out over the pool. "God! I'm sorry. I sound like him now," my chin jutted toward my dad. "I have a right to know what's going on here; a right to be considered, just as you do. I'm angry because that's my place to sit with you, to talk about college. That's *my* job—not his. Not just because I'm your father... but... I earned it, didn't I? Something you never did with me, Dad. You never gave me a second thought except in ridicule, or to beat me black and blue with your fists if the razor strap wasn't handy enough to suit you. You did nothing but belittle me and berate me."

I recognized the anger and bitterness in my voice but couldn't control it. "And you never apologized—for anything. So, I'm angry, yes. Do I hold it against you? Yes." I paused; maybe to find words that wouldn't bite quite so much, maybe just for effect—I'm not sure which. "I've done everything possible to be the father to him you never were for me. My son knows he can tell me anything. Ask me anything. He knows I won't laugh at him; I won't tell him he's stupid. He knows I respect him and trust him. I tell him I'm proud of him. That I love him."

I gawked at my son for what seemed like a full minute. Without looking at my dad, I finished, "He knows, because I don't just say it. I show it."

There was so much more to say, but my time was up. I pushed the timer across the glass surface to my father with the back of a hand, my eyes focused on the empty chair across from me.

Dad picked up the timer, cranked the dial, and put it down in front of himself in one swift motion. There was no hesitation, no deep breath to get started. "I'm not mad about anything. All I have to say is, I'm sorry if I've caused a rift here. I never intended to do that. I'm damn proud of the both of you." He nudged my arm to get me to look at him. When I didn't, he continued. "Am I sorry for the way I raised you? Yes. Certainly for the beatings. That's how things were done then. It's how your grandfather raised me. It was all I knew. You turned out all right though. You're still in one piece. As far as the ridicule, the belittling, it made you strong. You needed to be strong if you were queer."

He let out a short, soft sigh before he continued, "and I thought for certain you were. It broke my heart. I was scared for you, though. You needed to be tough inside, because you would never be tough on the outside. I didn't know how to talk about... those things. Do you think your grandfather explained anything to your uncles and me when we were kids? Not a chance. So what did we know? How could I know when a kid needs... certain information?"

"How about when they start asking questions. How about thinking back to when you were a kid," I barked at him.

Josh nudged me hard. "Not your turn."

My dad let out a soft sigh, and there was the slightest tinge of regret in his voice. "I'm sorry son. I really am sorry."

Okay. If I'm being totally honest, admittedly there are some obvious feminine qualities; the way I carry myself at times and some speech patterns. Maybe that would have given him reason for pause. But still...

We sat in silence as the timer ticked away. Josh picked up the bourbon and poured. I picked mine up and held the glass in front of my face, not quite able to look at either of them yet.

"I wanted your attention. I needed to know my dad was more than a prison guard, that you gave a shit. I didn't think you even wanted me. I thought you would've been happier if

I hadn't been born... If I were dead," my voice ended with a hoarse whisper, softer than anticipated. "You were the one. Mom admitted she never wanted kids. You insisted. Why?"

"Isn't that what life is about? Isn't that what's expected, what you're supposed to do? You grow up, you get married, you have children."

"For what? To treat us like shit?"

Josh snickered and nudged me.

A rueful smile crossed Dad's face. "Kids don't come with an instruction manual, you know. I did what I knew, the way I was taught."

That seemed a lazy recourse to me, but I didn't know how to respond without calling him such, the one thing he never was. I tossed my drink back and put the glass down on the table.

Josh hoisted his shot and held it waiting. My father refilled mine, picked up his own, and held it to Josh's. They waited. I finally reached out and, with the slightest hesitation, raised my glass.

Josh nudged my hand with his glass. "I love you Dad. You've been the best. You were there for me every time I needed you. I'll always need you. Don't you know that?"

Unbidden tears started streaming down my face. "I do, Sport."

"Sorry son; I fucked up," my dad said, giving his grandson a wink.

Josh laughed and reached out for a high-five, "All right, Gramp!"

"I promise I'll do better," my father clinked his glass on mine.

I turned my head to find him smiling at me and couldn't stop a grin from inching across my face. My glass ticked against theirs, and we tossed back our shots.

EXTRA $$$
Darlien C. Breeze

Money was tight. As usual. Hal griped about every expense. The fact that everyday living was on a never-ending upward spiral didn't help, "Myrna, you may have to get a job." Seeing the look on his wife's face, he quickly added, "Maybe just something part time. You know a little something extra to help make ends meet."

"And just when am I supposed to do this 'part time' work?" She looked at him is disbelief. "Between keeping your house immaculate, yes I said your house as you're quick to remind me, caring for the kids, need I remind you, your kids, your, yes your dogs and playing hostess to your endless poker parties tell me just when do I have time for another job?" she finished in a rush.

"Calm down. Don't get your bloomers in a twist. I thought maybe something you could do at home. I see these ads asking for home workers to stuff envelopes, make doll furniture and . . ." He stopped when he felt the room temperature drop. "Well, there must be something. Damn it, Myrna, we need extra money!"

"I see you've researched the job market Mr. Thorough. Have you also looked into how legitimate these job prospects are? Have you done your homework Mr. Know it All? Or are you, as usual, just going off half cocked, shooting your mouth off without looking into things?"

"Look Mike and his wife do okay. He makes about the same as I do but he said Sheila brings in a little extra doing alterations at home. Why don't you talk to her, see what she has to say?"

"Sheila, its Myrna. Do you have time to get together for coffee this morning? There's something I'd like to talk to you about. That's great. Come over when you can. The kids will be at school. We'll have the house to ourselves for a bit." She put the phone down and started for the laundry room. Stacks of sheets and unwashed school uniforms met her. Hal's kids didn't believe in wearing anything more than once and certainly wouldn't stoop to doing their own wash.

Later that morning, Sheila rang the doorbell. "What's up? You sounded stressed."

"That's putting it mildly. Hal wants me to get a part time job! Just when would I have time and what on earth would I do? He says you take in some sewing, do alterations is that true?"

Sheila laughed that raspy smoker's laugh she had. "Alterations. Yes, that's it. I alter men's anatomies, temporarily." Myrna looked blank. "The truth is, I turn a few tricks on the side. It brings in extra cash, Mike never questions me about it, and no one is the wiser. Plus no one get hurt."

"Tricks! You don't mean . . ." Myrna looked horrified.

"Of course I do. Oh, grow up, Myrna. This is not the dark ages. It's not like I'm hurting anyone."

"But how? I mean where do you get . . .them? How do you get away with it?"

"Easy. Once I caught on that several of the wives we know are doing it, then I just started offering my 'services' for a fee, of course. I spread a few bits of thread and some pins around for effect, and Mike's just happy for the money."

Extra $$$/Breeze

Sheila winked and said, "Let me explain the ins and outs of doing a cash business." Over the rest of the coffee and Danish, Myrna got a crash course on this particular home-based business opportunity.

The following week was the company dinner to present awards for outstanding sales. Hal made it clear that Myrna should look especially prosperous in a lavish new gown, even though they couldn't afford it.

At dinner Myrna caught the eye of Larry Turner, Hal's competition for sales, and made a special attempt to talk to him. He seemed very interested, especially when she rubbed his leg under the table with her stocking clad foot.

"Meet me at my house Wednesday at ten. We'll have the house to ourselves," she whispered to him later out on the balcony as they sipped champagne. "Bring five hundred dollars. I'll make it worth every penny."

On Wednesday, Myrna put fresh sheets on the bed and fresh towels in the bathroom. She had needles, pins, thread and a few shirt buttons along with scissors placed on a table in the den. First she was too hot, then too cold. Her palms were sweaty. "I can't go through with it. I can't do this. What if Hal catches me? What if I can't . . . perform?" she murmured to herself.

Larry was prompt. Afterward, he gladly gave Myrna five hundred dollars. "I'll be back for more of that."

Myrna heard the squeal of tires as Hal pulled into their driveway. He barely waited for the car to stop before he was out. He rushed into the house from the garage shouting, "Myrna, did Larry Turner come here this morning?"

"Good grief!" Myrna moaned, "he knows." She was sick to her stomach. How on earth . . .? Afraid to lie she stammered, "Yes, yes he came by about ten."

She was ready with the alteration story when Hal blurted,

"Did he give you five hundred dollars?"

Myrna felt faint. "Yes." She whispered. Her knees buckled. She sat down hard on the sofa.

"Good! I've been a nervous wreck. Larry asked to borrow five hundred from me yesterday. I couldn't let him know how strapped we are for money, so I loaned it to him. He said he'd come by this morning and pay it back. What a relief."

It took Myrna most of the evening to regain her equilibrium. Once back in control, anger replaced her sick feeling. Rage soon followed. What a fool I've been, she thought. What a naïve, stupid fool.

The next morning, after Hal and the kids were gone, she called Larry Turner's house. When his wife answered she said, in her most professional voice, "This is the Clark County Health Department, division of sexually transmitted disease, may I speak to Mr. Turner?"

"Mr. Turner's at work." Puzzled, she said, "This is Mrs. Turner may I help you?"

"It is imperative that Mr. Turner report to the Health Department immediately. Failure to do so could have dire results."

Hal was out of breath when he rushed into the house after work. He grabbed Myrna in a bear hug and twirled her around. "Get a sitter. We're going out for a special dinner to celebrate."

"What on earth, Hal. What's going on?"

He fanned several hundred-dollar bills in her face. "This!" He said. "Look at this!"

"Honey, stop. Take a breath. Tell me what you're talking about. Where did you get that money?"

"Okay, okay, but you have to promise never to breathe a word of this to anyone. I mean cross your heart and hope to die." He was grinning like a fool. "Larry, the jerk, came into my office this morning. He looked like hell. After he closed and locked the door, he told me about this call he got from the health department. Of course he told his wife it was some big mistake. He begged me to go down and take some tests in his place. He even gave me a thousand dollars to go. Can you believe it?"

"Wow! No I can't but what if . . .?"

"Oh he'll sneak off to a private doctor later, just to be sure. Meanwhile, let's celebrate! Remember, not a word of this to anyone, ever."

"Oh," she smiled, "you can trust me on that."

Throwaways—Perfect Match
(A Paranormal Thriller)
Garry Buzick

Chapter One

Dr. Omar Nadji glared over his surgical mask at his partner positioned at the edge of the operating room. Edward Pennington, known by most as Fast Eddy, nuzzled the three Igloo organ coolers between his imported Italian loafers while his fingers tapped an unknown song on the highly glazed tile wall. Although the operating room was well equipped for a free clinic, Omar had to have the best. He had a mission. Fast Eddy didn't have any formal medical training, but with the internet, he became a quick study on how to remove, store, and sell body parts. He focused on their acquisition and sale. His expertise as a computer hacker had given him access to all the organ waiting lists across the country, as well as all the blood banks, full to the brim with down-and-outs needing money.

Dr. Nadji, a new, young, brilliant surgeon, controlled the removal and, sometimes, the transplant portion of the business. These organs would soon be on their way to three Las Vegas hospitals. Substantial sums of cash awaited Eddy outside each of them. Cash was necessary, both for his unusual method of bookkeeping as well as to not leave

Writer's Bloc III

a paper trail. And, heaven forbid, in the unlikely event the transplant did not go well. These wealthy recipients had just been moved to the top of the waiting list.

Omar's patient, on full life support, brain dead, now just a grocery store of valuable organs. He made his first incision and asked, "So, how did this one die? Well, you know, oh, never mind," with irritation in his voice. No immediate answer from Eddy, just a shit-eating grin.

Eddy finally answered, "He must have hit his head pretty hard when he fell down. You know how these homeless drunks get. Probably knocked off a couple of bottles of cheap rotgut wine and lost his balance. You remember? Like your dad used to do. It's lucky that I was there right when it happened, or he would have ended with his life worth absolutely nothing. At least, this way we can pay to have him buried."

The unclaimed body count in Las Vegas had increased more than twenty-two percent from the previous year. No one wanted to claim the bodies.

With the hard economic times, some homeless were never claimed by the relatives. "Can you hurry; there're people getting anxious out there, and these coolers won't stay cold forever." Organ coolers had to be kept between one and ten degrees Celsius, with the ideal temperature not exceeding six degrees.

Omar grumped, "I just can't cut them out like you would a piece of steak. The connecting tissue has to be done precisely or there won't be any way to successfully transplant them. You know that." One of Doctor Nadji's evening nurses lifted the stainless steel bowl as he carefully placed the first kidney in it. Omar, disgruntled, said, "So, how did you create the nurses' passports and work visas, Eddy? Off the internet?"

The nurses were Chinese and didn't speak much English. They wouldn't have said anything even if they understood. They lived and worked in the U.S. illegally. One nurse scurried across the room to the tall stainless table and was met by Eddy, his cooler yawning for the bloody organ.

Eddy, ripping his surgical mask and scrubs off as he sped to the door, turned and said, "I'll be back in forty-five minutes for the others. Take the liver first. There's a millionaire just dying for a stiff cocktail," he laughed. Omar continued the surgery, not lifting his head or acknowledging Eddy as he left the room.

Chapter Two

My dream, or psychic vision, pulled me from a much more pleasant dream and jolted me upright. I sat in bed sweating, my heart pounding harder than after an aerobic workout. I didn't know their names or exactly where they were, but I already knew that I would have to find out.

It had been over a year since my divorce had been finalized from Angeni Tanis, or whoever she called herself now. The second-degree murder charges had been dropped, and I was a free man living in Las Vegas, Nevada. An abrupt change from the mountain splendor of Defiance, Colorado. But, a much needed change.

In search of closure, I visited a psychic who had left his business card on the front screen door of my meager new home in the Southwest. Still having twinges of regret over my lost marriage and, I guess, still coping with the fact that I had killed someone. It was ruled as self-defense, and, possibly, I should leave it at that.

I traveled a good distance from my home to my psychic appointment. I wondered about how I received the business card, dangling from my door, all the way across town. Ominous maybe, but it must have been something that I had to do. So, I went without significant hesitation. To get the full value, I didn't mention the 10% discount card for a palm

Writer's Bloc III

reading. And, I am a sucker for a deal. My mom, the coupon queen, would have been proud.

Not knowing what to expect, I entered the section of the strip mall that housed the psychic. I am not sure why I assumed she would be a woman, and was, indeed, greeted by a woman as I entered the shop. The lady, dressed in typical scarf-like clothing, welcomed me and asked that I take a seat in the divided-room reading area. The separation from the balance of the room minimalistic, Oriental room dividers with traditional Asian inspired art on each panel, one depicting a mountain shrouded on the lower third with dense fog and out of proportion trees rimming the edges. Chinese letters or symbols made with thick black brushstrokes embraced the lower portion of the panel.

I kept looking for a crystal ball on the small table positioned in the middle of the room. It had a glass top with randomly colored crystals strewn across it in no apparent pattern. But, no crystal ball. As I positioned myself in the less than comfortable wicker high back chair, the introduction lady appeared through invisible beads and announced that the "gay psychic" would now see me. I was a lesbian myself, so I didn't mind.

He entered extending his hand and said, "Welcome, I'm gay."

I shook his hand softly and said, "Nice to meet you, Gay, I'm Garrett Glenwood."

Gay said, "No, my name is Fred, and I'm gay."

I said, "Oh, I get it now, nice to meet you, Fred." Not the most picturesque name for someone that was a mystical person in my stereotypical perception. I didn't mention the 10% discount card, yet. I wanted to get a full reading. I asked Gay (maybe, I should just call him Psychic), which sounds better, "Did you know I was coming?" He plopped on his chair, without a turban or any normal headgear for a Swami.

"Of course, I knew you were a coming. Did you not read

the sign out front? I'm a psychic." He chuckled and expanded his already large mouth encompassing smile. I smiled back. I didn't believe him. There were charlatans in this field, and I'm not easily fooled. I had experience with psychics before. My ex-wife, though a pathological liar, I believe a true psychic. Her ability had never been facilitated by tarot cards or anything that resembled palm readings. Her ability rose from an occasional glancing meaningless handshake of someone that she probably didn't want to know anything about. Her visions more about their vile secrets than their love for puppy dogs. So, I had experience and would not be taken in.

 I scribbled some of the usual questions most people ask in a psychic reading, concerning love, the future, wealth and fame. I had, as a rule, given up on wealth and fame after leaving Colorado but had great interest in the future and, of course, my weak suits, love and women.

 Gay Psychic asked, "What would you like to learn about today?" His attitude was upbeat and casual. He seemed comfortable in his shoes or slippers as they appeared. I had no idea that you could buy slippers made from embroidered fabric with pointed toes on them. No sound came from the brash bells adorning the tip of his toes.

 I glanced around the room to see where his magic carpet might be, and said, "I am curious about my future in Las Vegas." I didn't mention I had just recently moved here. I didn't want to give too much away. He adjusted his hemp constructed bulky blouse, not a shirt, with the fabric belt tightly tied across his lower waist.

 "Why do you want to know whether the woman you asked out will become important in your life?" As he tilted his head and looked at me quizzically and, possibly, with suspicion.

 Shocked but pleased, I replied, "How did you know that was my second question?"

Writer's Bloc III

Still amused by me, he said, "Did you not read the sign on the front door? I am a psychic."

It was my turn to smile. I thought the reading was going well. "So, is she?"

The psychic leaned back in his unyielding protesting chair and said, "They are laughing at you and telling me that you should take a break from women for a while." His speech broken with an occasional nod, his vision leaving me to look at the group of spirits he spoke with. This in itself a little unnerving. "You have more spirit guides than most people I read. They do think you are amusing in your quest for women. They think that you should take a break. You may have more important things coming up."

He had no idea that I understood the need for so many spirit helpers. Shit happens when you are in my vicinity, and I'll take all the help I can get.

I thought, damn, I love women. What could be more important than that? He continued, "Usually people have one key spirit guide that comes up during a reading. You have at least five or six. The one speaking to me gives the impression he is their spokesperson, but the others aren't shy in voicing their desires."

"So, if I'm not supposed to be chasing women, what's this important thing I'm to do?"

He hesitated and nodded repeatedly to no one, at least, no one in the room, and spoke, "They say that you, like I, have an abundance of psychic ability, and they think you should try to develop it. When you can tap into their world, things, important things, will come to you and people will need your assistance."

"I already have a job." So what, if it's part time. I'm busy in my new town, still part tourist and an avid poker player. I didn't know if I believed him about the psychic ability thing, anyway. The ex had vast potential, but never willingly tried to gain knowledge from the other side. Hmm, could be possible.

The Oriental inspired hanging shelf containing the usual incense burner and Buddha decided to fall off the wall and crash noisily on the Oriental rug. Gay pressed back away from the table to retrieve the burning sandalwood incense and placed it on the table in front of me. I didn't much care for the fragrance, but too polite to ask him for a change. He said, "That's one of your spirits. He's rather spry." And a bit obnoxious.

I said, "I know he does crap like that all the time. Can you tell him to quit breaking stuff? It pisses me off when I have to try to fix something that I can't fathom how it in actuality works. Did I mention I'm not very mechanical."

"He's laughing at you. He's something of a character." Gay had such a good time with the spirits, talking about things that I couldn't understand, until I had to interrupt.

"What are you talking about?" Sometimes, when words leave your mouth, you regret their abandonment before they fall on the intended ear.

"Your foremost spirit guide tells me you are indeed a psychic, and the reason they are so plentiful is to help you develop your ability, and that is their plan for you. He says you were an amplifier to your ex-wife, but you have had the potential for a long time and that you just chose not to recognize it."

I didn't have a problem with exploring my psychic ability and tilted my head with a small frown and tipped eyebrow in acceptance. "So, what else should I know?"

"They said, 'All in good time.' They are leaving now, pulling away." He paused, "Well, I believe our reading is over."

"That was short. That's all I get?"

He tipped the front legs up from his chair and rocked backward and said, "Plus, you have one of those 10% off coupons that you're going to want me to use. So, you got a ninety percent reading. How's that?" He pushed his chair back and began to stand.

"How about you throw in one of those crystals?"

"Take your pick. They're genuine, you know." He escorted me through the invisible beads and directed me toward his assistant who looked for my payment. I thanked him and left lost in deep wondering what the spirit guides had in store for me as I traveled back to my home. Another larger puzzle, what would I do with a crystal? I glanced in my rear view mirror and gently tossed it into the bone-dry desert. Ashes to ashes.

One year earlier

Dr. Omar Nadji sat at his desk in the rear of the Desert Rose Clinic and sorted through large stacks of bills. Last week he had to let his accountant go. The economy in Las Vegas had dropped more than twenty percent each of the last two years, leaving the doctor swamped in bills from his student loans and millions of dollars awaiting payment for his state of the art clinic. His passion to treat the throwaways bleeding him, both financially and emotionally. He passed the bills from one stack to the other, placing some in file folders wondering how he could ever get caught up.

Sing Tao, his English-speaking nurse knocked politely on the half-open door and said, "There is a man wanting to see you, he's in the outer office. He is exceedingly insistent and says it's imperative that he sees you." She had barely finished the sentence when Edward Pennington barged into the room, glaring with his one eye at Sing and pushing her out the door as he simultaneously closed it.

Edward, Fast Eddy, never beat around the bush. His audacity and bulk crushed his way through life without waiting for many answers. "I have a proposition for you Doc, ah? Nehi."

Omar began to stand and said, "Excuse me, you don't

have an appointment and we are closed." Staring at his black eye patch, he said, "If you need some medical assistance you will have to come back tomorrow. We open at 7:00 a.m., but you will have to wait with everyone else. We do not take appointments. Kindly leave now."

Eddy, standing but not retreating, drew closer to Dr. Nadji, and his sure presence pressed him back into his chair. "You don't understand." Looking over his shoulder at the closed door, ears perked keenly. "I have a business proposition for you. I want to sell one of my kidneys, and I hear you are one of the finest young surgeons in Las Vegas." Dr. Nadji flipped a quick smile as Eddy continued. "And the coolest part is, I already have someone that wants it and will pay me, ah, us, $85,000 for it. Sweet, huh?"

Omar pulled a little closer to the lunatic, glanced at the huge stack of past due notices on his desk, and said, "You know, that's not how it works. You just can't sell your organs to the highest bidder." He suddenly pulled his focus to the eye patch that Eddy teasingly began to lift.

"Sure you can. If you know the right people," lowering his patch, thankfully, covering the fresh wound of his empty eye socket. "I think what you're doing down here is awesome, helping out runaways and the homeless and all. But, man, from the looks of it, you need some money, and I'm the guy that can make us rich," Eddy boasted.

Omar stood and walked to the door, locking it as if that would stop the voices from penetrating it. "What do you mean? You can make 'us' rich?"

"Easy, you've got the skills, and I have, ah, let's say, an extremely wealthy clientele. Just dying for an organ transplant." He laughed so hard, spittle misted the desk and computer screen. "See, I need some quick cash, you know how the casinos are, they may not bury you in the desert like they used to, but they sure as shit will rough you up and break a leg or two if they don't get their money. How about $25,000 to remove my kidney, and I'll take care of the rest?"

Omar, without hesitation, said, "I would make nearly that doing the operation at the hospital. Why would I do that?"

Eddy cackled, "No taxes, straight cash. No insurance crap to deal with. Plus, it doesn't look like you have a long line of paying customers out front. Ha. That's why you'll do it. And there's more. If this one works, well, the opportunities are endless. So, what do you say, we got a deal?"

Dr. Nadji nodded.

The Selection
A.L. Campbell

Teko balanced on the balls of his feet, arms relaxed in the ready position. The stance allowed swift movement in any direction. After a morning spent training first-level Narakian warriors, those in the ten to twelve year age range, in the art of Kochu combat, he gloried in focusing his master skills against an equal.

Melin crouched dead fast and swung her right leg out at the same time as the *slit* gripped firmly in her right hand, a move designed to knock an opponent from his feet before opening up a wound wherever the blade contacted the body.

Anticipating some such move, Teko leapt a full second before the *slit* whistled past where his belly had been. The jump took him above the range of any of Melin's appendages. He spun before landing and snapped a kick to her head that caught only hair as she ducked away. Calculating his next move, Teko failed to notice the chimes until his sparring partner's attention drifted from the fight.

The distinctive tones called all unemployed warriors to the main arena for Selection. Already, others in the training room headed for the corridor.

"I must go," Teko said, "so we'll finish this tomorrow."

"Unless you are chosen," Melin reminded him.

"As you say." Teko nodded and walked off, suppressing a grin, as he had no intention of working for anyone. The only job even mildly tempting to him was the one of Kochu instructor, which the woman he walked away from already held.

A shove from behind proved he'd lowered his guard too much. He grabbed the door frame to stop his forward momentum before his face could plow into it.

"Oh, sorry," a younger man said with a laugh.

Teko knew he wasn't, not missing the collaborative looks that passed between the man and Tayn, Teko's lifelong rival.

"Let's go, Akyn," the co-conspirator urged.

Annoyance caused Teko's muscles to tighten and he forced them to loosen. A Kochu master should know better and he did, but something about Tayn clashed with him, set him on edge.

Following the others at a slower pace, Teko utilized the time to reclaim his calm. Although the elders expected them to come directly when called, he knew it would take time to gather those scattered throughout Naroke.

In the main arena, Teko leaned back against the wall and concentrated on being inconspicuous. He didn't want to be there and had no intention of being selected, the process by which Kochu warriors were hired out to the Gentarans. Today, the Narakian elders had summoned *all* eligibles, not just the masters, which made that goal more attainable. Only a high-level Gentaran could demand that.

When all had arrived, roughly one hundred men and women surrounded the central combat mat, awaiting the call to demonstrate their skills.

The itchy feel of eyes upon him, Teko panned the faces and made a mental note of the two men watching him—the same pair that accosted him earlier—but didn't acknowledge that he saw. He merely kept them in his peripheral vision as they waited.

Being of like age, he and Tayn had competed all their lives, but never became friends. Teko believed Tayn harbored too much jealousy for that, because he could never best Teko in combat unless he let him, which, in fact, he did—during Selection. Besides, he had no use for friendship even if the other man had pursued one.

Nervousness showed on some of the younger Narakians, released somewhat when a hooded figure entered the arena with two elders. A feeling of foreboding crawled up Teko's back. Hooded meant the person didn't want to be recognized, either because of their rank or for nefarious reasons—trouble either way. If the latter, he or she had to convince the elders otherwise. The cloaked individual sat in the first row of seats, flanked by the standing elders.

Called forward two at a time, the Narakians fought hand-to-hand until one person immobilized the other or admitted defeat. No blades were used during Selection, but Teko knew recordings of special weapons training sessions could be reviewed on request.

"Teko and Akyn," announced Mayvon, the female elder.

Teko pushed off from the wall and approached the square. He deposited his shoes and shirt on the floor before crossing the lined border of the mat.

The smirk on Akyn's face made him suspicious. His gut clenched. *Those two are up to something. But what?* Teko remained alert.

"Begin," came the order to start.

He could overtake Akyn any time he wanted, but chose not to. He'd worked hard at appearing to bend under pressure at these events. Not winning, or not winning well, had kept him from being chosen so far, so when he left the weaker man an opening, it surprised him that Akyn didn't take advantage of it.

Writer's Bloc III

"You're getting weak," Teko grumbled low into the other man's ear as they locked arms about each other.

"You're the one that wants to appear that way," came the rebuttal, "but we won't let that happen this time."

In a move that falsely showed his opponent in control, Teko broke away. The knot in his stomach tightened. Until now, no one ever cared or commented that his performance on the Selection mat failed to demonstrate his true expertise. His concentration faltered in a moment of panic at being exposed, long enough for a full strike to hit his shoulder. Flinching at the sharp pain, he attempted to refocus.

It didn't work. Instead of allowing that sloppiness to take him out, the anger overwhelmed him, and in two moves, *Akyn* went down, quickly admitting defeat.

Stupid, stupid, stupid, Teko chastised himself and returned to his position at the wall. *Get control.* Tayn's grin made him frown and he closed his eyes to block it out.

Teko blanked his expression and felt the cells in his body shift as they regenerated. Within minutes, all pain ceased. He knew his skin had paled to resemble the color of the wall, while his hair remained light brown. Hair color took a full day to change. This ability is what kept Narakians alive long after the toxins of Ryllex, their home planet, killed all others.

Ten warriors remained when Mayvon called Teko and Tayn to the mat. Teko's last two opponents, neither master-level, had been too unskilled to lose to, the match-ups suspiciously unequal. Even the moves he practiced to throw the match out-performed them. Vowing to remain centered, Teko assumed beginning stance.

The fight began. The two tested each other with standard moves. Neither dominated. Tayn attacked, only to back off.

As the match went on, Teko's frustration built. Finally, he swiveled away from a kick and moved in close for a grab.

"What do you think you're doing?" he asked.

Blocking Teko's punch, Tayn twisted away and snickered. "Getting you out of Naroke. For good."

"Why?" They circled. Teko stayed on the balls of his feet. Tayn feinted, giving him an opportunity he didn't take. *I won't be lured in.*

"I'm on to you." Tayn lunged with a fist to Teko's chest.

He absorbed the punch that wasn't as hard as it should be and then dropped to his knees, with a bit of acting, as if it was.

That incited Tayn. The subsequent elbow smash to the face held nothing back. He wrapped his arms around Teko's neck and leaned in to say, "We want you gone. Everyone wants you gone." Then, as if realizing he had the upper hand, Tayn faked a receiving knee drive under the arm and into the side and then fell to the mat as if tripped.

For just a second, the other man's words saddened Teko, but then, he let it fuel his determination. As if drenched in ice water, a coldness swept over him head to foot. His perception sharpened and all moves became more precise, even while made to look sloppier. His calculations put him in the right place to receive the attacks Tayn tried to hold back on, but before the other man regrouped, Teko conceded the match to him.

Frigid disdain filled Teko as he stood and walked off, never dropping eye contact with Tayn. In his opponent's, he saw murder.

Whole once more, Teko found himself called to the interview room with several others, including Tayn. He hadn't wanted to make it that far and reminded himself that, even if offered the contract, he could refuse and go about his business. Sitting on a hard-backed wooden chair, he wondered if the elders stayed in the room to advise, or even speak for, the mysterious employer, or if he or she planned to speak for themselves.

Sometime after Tayn departed with a final dagger stare of hate, the door opened and Mayvon came out. "Teko," she greeted him before gesturing to the door, "you may go in."

The door clicked shut behind him, without the old woman. Seated at the head of a long table, the hooded figure waved a gloved hand to the closest seat.

"Please, sit," a male voice said.

Teko did and waited.

"Subject, Teko Naraki," the man said casually and consulted the tablet laying before him.

Teko knew his bio, limited as it was, would indicate his special skills, including the different appearances he'd perfected as well as his combat record.

"I see you are very skilled at camouflage," the deep voice stated.

"No more than any other Narakian." Teko downplayed his abilities. No sense leading the man to believe him eager when he clearly wasn't. He studied the dark brown hood, attempting to see the face within.

The man angled his head to prevent it, not needing to see the subject of his interview, evidently. He continued. "I also see that you have won more than your fair share of Kochu matches."

Teko didn't answer. It occurred to him the man might attempt to read his mind, a futile exercise on a Narakian that arrogant Gentarans still tried.

"And yet, you did not win today."

"No." His tone remained as even as the interviewer's.

The man studied the tablet again, before saying, "I found your acting today very convincing."

That shook Teko, but he strove not to show it. "What makes you think I was acting?"

"I have studied the Kochu warriors and their moves. I know a feint when I see one. What I wonder is why?"

Dead silence reigned.

"Do you wish to dishonor the contract the Narakians have with the Gentarans?"

Voice still level, Teko answered, "I have done nothing to dishonor the contract. Narakians are not required to accept service, so an offer refused will not be deemed dishonorable." Although he couldn't see the man's face, it felt to Teko as if his words amused him. He dampened the irritation that thought provoked.

"I'm seeking someone to perform a special task," the man said seriously, as if tired of playing games.

It not being a request, Teko didn't respond. *Make your offer or dismiss me*, he thought.

"The task will take that person off planet and may last to the end of the contract period."

All contracts terminated at the end of the generation that began with the Narakian settlement on Gentara, if not sooner. The statement, against his better judgment, piqued Teko's interest. He'd always wanted travel and adventure, but only on his own terms.

"Who will this person work for?" he found himself asking.

"No one. He will report, and be accountable, only to me. All expenses will be paid from a private account until the job is done or the contract expires."

Tempting, but there's always a downside. "What are the negatives?"

"No one can know where you are or what you are doing. And most of all, no one can know who you are working for."

Although those conditions didn't bother him, having no one in his life to tell since his parents' death years ago, his instinct warned that something wasn't right. "I couldn't do anything against the code. I don't believe I am your man." He started to rise, considering his words a refusal even though the job hadn't officially been offered.

"Wait."

Teko stood before his chair and waited.

"Nothing I ask of you will be contrary to any laws. You have no family among the Narakians. You don't appear to have many, if any, friends, either. Yet, you do have the skills I need. None will question your absence. What other concerns do you have?" The words contained no inflections to indicate any emotion was involved.

What he says is all true, Teko thought. *And, he sounds convincing; I'll give him that.* Only one real obstacle remained. "I do not want to work for anyone." He stepped away, expecting that to be the end of the interview.

"Do you think Tayn Naraki will suit me for this task?"

Teko halted once more. "Maybe. He has both family and friends here, but he, like any Narakian, would serve you honorably." Thinking about the other man doing this job brought a sour taste to his throat. While it would put distance between the two of them, it would also give Tayn a semblance of the life Teko had always wanted for himself. The jealousy that thought provoked made him uncomfortable and, before he could stop the words leaving his mouth, he asked, "What if I want the job?"

"Do you want the job with the conditions I have stated?"

Teko's heart raced, filled with surprise and excitement, before slowing to a calm resolve. "I do," he said, and a feeling of rightness came with saying it.

"Then," the unknown man solemnly said, "I select you."

The Love That Transcends
Alejandro E. Czeisler

Sweat pouring, pulse racing, my chest felt as if my heart was being ripped out. Pungent hospital smells and bitterness in my mouth were making me sick, as sounds of whispering and crying echoed in my head. Grotesque images flashed in my mind and feelings of anguish, anger and emptiness haunted me. I had to get away. Suddenly, racing towards me, a beam of light grew closer, brighter, and a horrifying sound kept screaming at me. I clenched my fists in mid air and tried to scream back, but nothing came out. All sounds were hushed and the glare vanished. A million tiny luminaries filled the air and gathered to envelop and lift me away, comforting and dissolving my pain until I finally gave up all consciousness.

    I awoke to a gentle spring breeze coming through the dormer window of my attic room. It was a sunny day, filled with the scent of honeysuckle, sounds of rustling leaves and faint twittering of birds. It reminded me of a Sunday morning, when I was a child and my family lived in the loft apartment of a Victorian rooming house in East Providence. I sat by the old desk and looked out the window. The tire swing Father had hung on the oak in our tidy backyard was swaying back and forth. Was I still dreaming? It had been a long time since I felt this much happiness and peace. I had no idea why or even how I got home. I chose not to remember.

Although my family gave me the advantages of a good education and all the things they never had growing up, my childhood was lonely. Father crewed on a fishing boat out of Narragansett and was out to sea for weeks at a time. Mother sewed at home until all hours of the night, and Grandma, who had crossed the Atlantic with Father, was always busy with housework. They kept their hardships and painful memories of war very much to themselves. It wasn't until Randy and his family moved downstairs that I felt I finally had a friend to confide in.

I heard approaching footsteps. Grandma pushed the door open with a tray and entered, singing a Hungarian nursery tune she serenaded me with in my childhood. The air filled with rich aromas of cold coffee-milk and homemade Dobos Torta. She turned to me and said "Happy birthday, sleepyhead. Should I sing for you some more? But look at you in your tugboat pajamas. You're not even ready." Placing the food on the desk, she faked a stern look. "Didn't I warn you that someday you would be late for your own funeral?" She broke out in laughter.

"For me, Grandma?" I asked.

She rolled her eyes in mock disbelief. "So you know some other grandson I would bake for?" She smiled but then fell silent for a long moment. As she continued, her voice broke. "It's so good to have you home, like when you were our little boy." She paused again. I felt embarrassed as she clumsily tried to wipe the tears welling up in her eyes. "Enough of this nonsense. I am acting like a fool, crying when I should be happy. You hurry up and get dressed. We are due in church in less than an hour. Randy is going to be here any moment."

As I ate my cake, I felt tears spilling down my cheeks, but I could not understand why. My birthday was back in September, and when did Grandma learn to speak so well?

Dad insisted that we only speak English in our household.

Speaking Magyar was too much like looking back. This edict was hardest on Grandma whose English was so bad as to render it comical. The only exceptions were when she would sing me to sleep with one of her lullabies from back home or occasionally, late at night, when she and Mom thought I could not hear them, they would quietly reminisce or even joke in Hungarian. I longed to understand what they were saying, to join in, to belong to the secret world they shared.

My best suit and tie were neatly hung in my closet. I got dressed quickly and climbed down to the living room. I was thinking of Grandma when I came face to face with Randy. I hadn't seen him in ages and I couldn't take my eyes off him. He seemed so young, like I remembered him, before I went to college and we lost touch.

"David, good to see ya buddy," Randy said. "Are you and Granny ready for the funeral?" The memories of my nightmare overwhelmed me. My face went pale. I realized someone dear to me had died. "It's okay. Don't worry so much, little brother," Randy said, placing his right hand on my shoulder and giving me one of those broad, confident grins I remembered so well. "Besides, they can't start the ceremony without you, can they?"

Randy was 12 and I was almost 11 when his family took the rooms below ours. From the day we met, we became inseparable. I was a scrawny little kid with thick glasses and making fun of me had become the official pastime of my schoolmates. Since I had no brothers or sisters, he took me under his wing. He taught me to play stickball and stand up for myself and I helped him with his math homework so his father would not get mad and beat him. In our free time we did our best to scandalize the old ladies and frustrate the shopkeepers in our block. We adopted each other. By high school, we were closer than real brothers. He understood my loneliness, even though he had an older sister, 13-year-old Elizabeth.

Writer's Bloc III

Unlike Randy, Betsy took a long time to warm up to me. I was too shy to speak to her and she had no time to figure me out. Keeping house and filling the shoes of both mother and sister in their household, there had been no time for her to play with dolls or socialize with other girls. In school, most kids thought her odd and guys stayed away. There was an unfeminine directness in her manner, as well as a style no one ever understood. I adored her for it, from a distance. It wasn't until I was thirteen, facing the frightful prospect of my first school social, that I worked up the nerve to share my heart. I asked her to teach me how to dance and while I held her close in my arms, I promised I was going to marry her some day. She didn't laugh at me. She didn't say no. She just smiled and said to ask her again when I was taller than she was.

Randy and his mom got in the front of his dad's old Ford Falcon. Grandma and I got in the back and we drove away. As we neared the church, I could recognize faces I hadn't seen since I was a kid. There was Charlie, the corner grocer, Mrs. O'Bryan, my homeroom teacher, our old pastor, Reverend Wilkins and many more, including some of the older kids from my high school that had gone to Vietnam. As we walked to church from the parking lot, one by one they all came to me, shook my hand and expressed their happiness to see me.

I was about to enter the building when the nightmare came back. I froze in my tracks. I knew whose funeral it was. It was Betsy's. It was my wife's. Growing up together, the fiber of our characters had been woven in to a single cloth. All that I was, and all that I ever hoped to be, had no meaning without her.

I could almost feel the warm delicate moisture of her soft lips on mine when we first kissed the night of her senior prom. I found her in our backyard, lying in the grass, looking at the stars. She had been crying all day. None of the young men asked her to go to the prom. I brought her a blooming red rose from Grandma's garden and, kneeling next to her, I said, "Don't you know you are beautiful, and that I will love you to the day I die?"

We had gotten married right after college and, after years of trying to get pregnant, we finally succeeded with a little help from science. Then came the complications. She left me as she gave birth to our daughter, even though she had promised we would never part. As I drove home from the hospital, I approached a railroad track. I could hear the train whistling, trying to stop, and then nothing. A crucial event was missing from my memory.

It was too much for me to handle. My legs gave out from under me, but Randy caught me and said in his best brotherly tone, "Be strong now. She is waiting for you inside. You don't want her to see you looking like this."

Grandma rushed to me and embraced me tenderly in her shaking arms as she spoke through her sobs, "My sweet, sweet boy. It's all over now. All pain is behind you. Go in now. It's time for your birthday."

Nothing made sense anymore. Was this my wife's funeral or my birthday? It was then I realized Grandma had not been speaking English to me at all. She had been talking to me in Hungarian and I understood her perfectly.

I walked through the doors, down the center aisle. The sanctuary was flooded with a light that beamed from the stained glass windows all around. A choir of angels filled the air with heavenly melodies and harmonies. Standing by the altar was Betsy, alive, all dressed in white, waiting for me with open arms. I ran as fast as I could, and when we embraced, it was as if we had never parted at all. "Happy birthday, my love!" she whispered softly in my ear.

I turned around. The church was filled with all the people who had touched my life. There was Randy, who had a fatal motorcycle accident during my senior year of college.

Writer's Bloc III

He was sitting next to his mother who had succumbed to cancer when he was two years old. Grandpa and Grandma were together, holding hands, finally reunited after she had passed away last year. They were all dead, yet they were all here, wishing me happy birthday.

"I don't understand," I said, looking at that unexpected congregation.

Then Grandma stood up and spoke. "This is your birthday present, my beloved boy. You are home now, and you can stay if you wish." My heart was caught in a whirlwind of emotions. I was happy, frightened, bereaved and dumbfounded.

I turned back to Betsy and managed to say, "I thought this was your funeral, my love. I could not bear to face life without you."

She gently pressed her right index finger, sealing my lips and said, "You were about to take you own life but I could not let you. I couldn't bear to see you suffer that way, none of us could, so we all decided to bring you home early and give you a glimpse of your own funeral, but from our perspective. In Heaven we prefer to call it your birthday.

"Now you have a hard decision to make, my beloved. You can stay with us, or go back and raise our baby. My heart won't allow me to ask you to go. You are the love of my life and Heaven isn't Heaven without you, but the decision has to be yours. I will endure the wait if you decide to return. I only have one request, my love. If you do go back, I want you to name our daughter Angela."

I am sitting behind the wheel of my BMW. The car is on the railroad tracks and a train is fast approaching, whistling furiously, and screeching on its tracks, trying to stop. I step on the accelerator and the train narrowly misses me. Trembling, I pull into the nearest gas station and get myself a cup of coffee. It is awful stuff, but it is good to be alive and be able to taste bad coffee. I drink it in small sips. I have a lot to think about.

After a while, I get in the car and slowly drive back to the hospital. Entering the maternity ward to see my daughter, it occurs to me I have a new purpose. I will raise her and protect her as best I can, and also tell her about her mother. Keeping alive the memories of all the people I loved, along with their stories, I will pass on the love that transcends all generations.

My parents walk towards me and embrace me together. "We feel so worried about you," says Mom. "When you left, you looking so desperate, we thought, you do something foolish."

Father cut in, "But you ok now."

One of the nurses brings me my baby and says, "Here is your daughter, sir."

"What you going to name her?" asks Father.

"I don't know. She has Betsy's eyes."

Then my mother interrupts, "You see the little baby daughter. She is little angel Betsy left here on earth to look after you, son."

"Angela, I'll call her Angela."

The Dyatlov Incident
Douglas Davy

Yuri Yudin focused on the inn's garret room window that faced the infamous Otorten Mountain Passage in the northern Ural range. The window sill bore brown burn-track fingerprints of time and cigarettes long forgotten. "I should have gone with them." Yuri crushed his cigarette amid precariously high ashen debris. "My one question for God would be, what really happened to my friends that night in 1959?"

American journalist Stewart Jackson shifted uncomfortably in his hard wooden chair.

"This seems a sentinel place. You're the only surviving member of a disastrous skiing expedition."

"It tortures me to return, watch, and wait here for hours each day. My long dead friends are gone, but here I stand, watching where they last skied out of this village," Yuri reflected. "Afterward, I worked at Ural Polytechnic Institute until I retired to move back to Vizhai." Yuri's voice, lost in cigarette smoke, carried the echo of time. "Dyatlov promised to telegram the Institute by February 12, as soon as the team returned from Otorten Mountain."

"I'm 68 years old." Yudin stood in the posture of a younger man. "Heart surgeries haven't broken my spirit, but they tell me I've got survivor's guilt." His deep-set eyes revealed this internal struggle. "What really happened that cold February 2nd night in 1959? Many of us still search for answers.

"We worked, lived, and trained hard as a team experienced in long ski tours and mountain expeditions." Yuri spoke toward the mountain. "This route was Category III. Even for Igor Dyatlov, this trek would earn us a higher degree in sports acheivement." He put his head in his hands. "Why did I get sick that day?" he whispered.

"Did doctors ever find why you were ill?" Stewart Jackson knew his survivor's story. He knew the deaths of Yuri's nine companions, fifty years before, remained one of the Ural's deepest mysteries. The government concealed Yudin's true identity for many years to keep the incident quiet. Baffled investigators in 1959 simply stated, "The group died as the result of a 'compelling unknown force,'" then abruptly closed the case as "Highly Classified" until the early 1990s.

Yudin looked up. "Doctors put it down as some sort of virus. I felt ill the night before, but Dyatlov had pushed us hard all day. Our bodies collapsed early, our muscles felt it, but we slept excited. We planned an early start, journey over the mountain pass, return here when the trek ended, and celebrate. We'd have ridden back from Vizhai in triumph."

Yuri sighed. "I felt weak that morning. Not even strength to put clothes on. Dyatlov decided to leave me behind. Reluctant, weak, burning with fever, I agreed. The team left me to sleep it off." Yuri lit another cigarette, rose, and paced as he spoke.

"I'm haunted to explain what happened that night." Yudin's gaze moved back like darkening shadows on the mountain and inhaled the smoking ember of his memories. "Dyatlov led to the Kholat-Syakhl location. Not to lose distance covered, he must have decided to camp that mountain slope. Dyatlov expected to return a few days later than planned.

He wasn't aware, but in the local Mansi language, Kholat-Syakhl means 'The Mountain of the Dead.'" Yuri sighed, causing the window to fog briefly.

"A snowstorm whipped up, but it hadn't prevented good spirits. They pitched tents around 5:00 p.m. investigators decided from diaries, photos developed from rolls of film, and cameras found lying amid debris and abandoned belongings in the collapsed tents.

"The film wasn't exposed to any radiation that we know of. Cameras, in normal fashion, took shots of team activities."

Yuri set a brown accordion file on the kitchen table. He produced from it yellowed, simple photographs of young men and women setting a barracks tent in the snow. "Just enough late afternoon light to allow these shots." His haunted eyes looked through the pictures. "After government files opened, I was able to have these. When I touch them I can feel my friends." His smile faded to become stoic and serious. "If their fate was sealed or affected somehow by radiation, why didn't the film get exposed?"

"They look like they were having a good time," Stewart volunteered.

"Look at Georgyi. He was always clowning..." Yuri laid his hand over the picture for a moment. A hint of a smile flitted across his face.

"At the funerals they all looked a deep brown tan, or sunburned, or something...their hair had turned grey...they might even have been blinded by whatever it was." Yuri took a long drag on his cigarette and blew out the puff.

"And this?" Yuri pulled a small glass jar from the cabinet, unscrewed the lid, and displayed a coil of tent fabric. "This long, heavy zipper was torn from the front of their tent... all the way around... from the inside out."

Stewart easily pulled the zipper down six inches and then closed it again. "Did you have any trouble opening that?" Yuri asked.

"Not a bit." Stewart responded.

"Then why leap up in a panic to rip the tent open? What stopped this zipper from gliding open in 1959?"

Stewart's blank stare offered no answers.

"All nine were in underwear, barefoot, or with a single sock or boot. Why race out into sub-zero temperatures without coats or boots or skis? Few made it more than a kilometer and a half down the slope. Fifty degrees below zero killed them quickly.

"Investigators let me keep the zipper and photos." Yuri put the zipper back. "Why did I survive it all?"

Stewart groped for something, "Maybe you needed to tell their story."

"You don't realize...this gnawing inside me. Years... plagued by questions. It always starts the same...

"I remember waking up confused by the dark outside. Where was I? What time was it? My head was woozy from sleeping most of the day. I'd been out cold. I stumbled down the bathroom hall, then back to my room. It felt all wrong somehow." He touched the window. "I looked toward the direction my friends had traveled."

"I'd stumbled awake to see them depart. So much laughing and talking clamor outside as they readied to leave. Heartsick to be left out, I watched at the window. Equipment checked, I tried to wave, but no one looked back.

"Georgyi generally skied first to break the trail. The team found natural places behind him as he led out of the village. They moved out of sight from my window. The last time anyone would ever see them alive."

On the Mountain, 1959

The long day's trek was arduous. They set up camp on the wintery front range of

Kholat-Syakhl, a mountain next to Otorten. Dyatlov

chose the spot. They could've detoured 1.5 kilometers down the mountain to a forest, where shelter from the harsh elements existed.

"Why stop here for the night?" Nicolas Thibeaux-Brignollel voiced her opinion. Other members of the party held their activity.

"This spot is too open," Yury Doroshenko exclaimed.

Lyudmila Dubinina added, "The snowfall might increase. This spot will bury us if winds kick up."

"We'd have more cover in the woods," Rustem Slobodin said.

"I think like soldier. We're too exposed here," Spoke Alexander Zolotarev, at 37 the oldest member of the team. "In a fight, there's better shelter in the trees."

Dyatlov had decided. "This is the spot for us," he proclaimed. "We are a Category III team with Mastery of all terrains. Let us camp this mountain slope. Any group of adventurers can hide in the trees." Dyatlov paused. "All right, I'll bow to the wishes of the majority." He stood with arms crossed. "Does it really matter where we camp?"

"Fighting about this will only make us more weary," Georgyi sighed.

The team looked one to the other. Then, with a nod and a shrug, turned experienced hands to making camp for their fateful rendezvous.

"The sooner we set up camp, the sooner we can eat," Alex Kolevatov acknowledged.

The group broke out in laughter. "You're right, Alex," Georgyi added. "We must trust your stomach to pick the spot."

Tents were erected amid fun and photographs. They moved inside to sit on sleeping bags. Small camp stoves nourished them with soup, while bread, cheese, and hard salami appeared from food packs. Some made notes in diaries, and all smiled to be warm and fed. There was barely floor space to comfortably huddle within this barracks tent.

"Watch who you're pushing. I nearly spilled my soup on you." Zina Kolmogorova balanced her meal on her knees.

"I got jostled by Lyudmila. At least, she's got some soft padding," Georgyi quipped.

"You get too interested in that jostling business, and I'll punch you in the nose, Georgyi Krivonischenko. Keep your body parts to yourself," Lyudmila snapped back.

"Alright children," Dyatlov tried to sound stern, "you must learn to play nicely with one another." He surveyed the tent. "Lyudmila and Zina, please help gather traces of food and stash them. The men won't mind if you go squeezing in and around them."

"You can squeeze in and around me all you want," Georgyi said. All were in good spirits as activities quieted down.

"No trouble sleeping tonight." Igor Dyatlov pulled up his sleeping bag. "Georgyi and Yury, the lightest sleepers, are by tent opening so nothing gets in or out without them knowing." He sat up for one last check. All were nestled into their down bags. Their coats and sweaters were pillows. Breathing rates were slowed. "We will all soon sleep the sleep of the dead," he mused, pulled up the bag, and drifted into sleep.

Reflections

Yuri's window-gazing continued, even after nightfall. He spoke over his shoulder.

"Another group camped 50 kilometers south of them that night. Their leader reported they all saw strange 'bright orange flying spheres' floating in the night sky off in the direction of Kholat-Syakhl."

The Spheres, 1959

Late that cold February night, high over Mount Kholat-Syakhl, bright-metallic orange spheres flashed their lights.

The largest was a full 48 feet across. The rest ranged in size from 24 to 12, to 6, to 3 feet in diameter. Sparks of light streamed soundlessly between them as they zipped and flew about over the team's quiet campsite.

Sharp pointed rays of purple light shot from the center of the largest sphere. Five of the smallest orbs slowed from erratic flying patterns in and around the rest and hovered directly over the main tent. They swarmed, sparkled, and floated tightly together like metallic orange fireflies. Under the watchful observation of the larger spheres, the small swarm slowly descended. Their glow passed through the tent's ceiling material where the spheres hovered, cloistered inside.

The skiers slept oblivious to their visitors. Cold, intense, violet-white luminescence manifested inside the tent. Over sleeping skiers, blinding light porcupined radiant blue-purple radiation. Spheres, suspended in fluid light, filled the tent with an effulgence of radiation in pinpoint-quilled rays.

Time suspended. Moments stretched into silent minutes. The spheres maneuvered fluid and weightless, hovering just above the sleeping faces. Nestled into down-filled retreats hours ago, Dyatlov and team members stayed collapsed in sleep.

The frigid, biting intensity of Russian winter in February waited silently outside. Only thin tent walls restrained its appetite from gnawing upon their human warmth. Even the light snow had gradually stopped. No breeze stirred the cold night as temperatures chilled to almost 50 degrees below zero.

The Awakening, 1959

Simultaneously, the group awoke with a shock. The visitors' blinding light caused searing internal pain. The team jolted awake, immersed in an unknown terror. Their pain found voice. Every throat screamed reactions. Skiers writhed upon the floor in agony, their bags providing no shelter. Pinpoints of light stabbed through fabric to elicit pain from every cell.

Dyatlov screamed above the shreaking cacophony of pain filling the tent, "Get out! Crawl out of your bags. Get away from this tent, now!" He shouted to Georgyi and Yury, "Open the tent!" Nine bodies pushed their mass toward the tent flap as skiers scrambled out of bags.

The light spheres packed the tent with their presence, their density, and their radiation.

Instant sunburn-like pain throbbed on any exposed flesh. Searing light burned, probed, and forced itself through fabric weave pores. It shot through long underwear like hot needles.

Georgyi and Yury, closest to the tent flap, rushed to open their escape route. Other members crawled, snaked, and weaved toward them. They huddled low and away from the firebrands glowing in their tent's apex, hiding from the painful sphere-light. As searing brilliance grew exponentially, the level of pain grew with it.

"Don't look at the light!" Dyatlov screamed in warning. Eyes burned as if they looked directly at the sun or into the energy arc of a welder without protective masks. Screaming intensified. Bodies clutched and pushed each other to escape new pain.

"Let us out of here!" Lyudmila shrieked. A few groped for shreds of warmer clothes, but the intensity and pain of the blinding light distracted selectivity. The tent zipper locked tight.

"The zipper won't budge!" Georgyi finally found strength to rip open a tear in fabric next to the zipper. "Help me, Yury," he screamed. Dyatlov, groped through the bodies to press forward and get his hands into the tear. Three men ripped together. Finally, fabric tore away until they flung back the zipper. Still closed tight, it hung by a small strip from the tent flap.

"Run," screamed Dyatlov. Near naked bodies vomited into the cold through the torn canvas. "Get away from the pain of those lights."

"Let us out!" Lyudmila pushed forward over other pain frenzied team members stumbling to escape. Exited in panic, their canvas retreat collapsed. The clustered spheres regrouped and hovered bright overhead.

"I can't see," Zina screeched in panic.

"That light blinded us," Rustern hollered. Others agreed. "...And burned us...Even in this snow, I feel burning on my skin."

"Run for the trees. Get away from here." Dyatlov stumbled down the mountain slope. All tried to focus night vision in the starlight. "Head for the edge of the forest."

In an instant flash, the cluster of light spheres lifted off and scattered in all directions. Their diminished sizes faded toward the horizons.

"Good God, what were they?" Georgyi stomped a path in the snow toward dark forest shadows below. The team, some barefoot, several in stocking feet, stumbled to follow as they moved away from the tent. Few had extra clothes. The cold frost giant of Russian winter clawed at their exposed flesh and squeezed out body warmth with minus 50degree fingers.

"Shit, I'm cold," Georgy grumbled as he reached a large pine. He'd followed its blurred image, even with his vision nearly gone. "Over here. A big tree. Follow my voice."

"This tree will help block us from the tent." Dyatlov looked back. One of the smaller bright orange spheres had reappeared to hover 50 meters overhead. He said nothing to the group.

"My face burns." Alexander touched his cheek.

"Anyone have matches?" Georgyi asked. He'd pulled together some pine kindling. "We need a fire or we're really done for."

"I have some," Lyudmila said. She'd grabbed her faux fur coat and hat when scrambling out of the tent. Georgyi started the small fire. The team quickly huddled around it. Bare feet, stockings, and lightweight underwear afforded little protection from this cold.

"I think the larger spheres have vanished. The smaller spheres seem to have moved off as well," Dyatlov announced. "Making our way back to the tent is the only survival option. There's little time left before hypothermia will really set-in. We're already pushing it." He looked around the shivering group.

"You're right," Georgyi said. "I'll climb this tree…see if I can spot any lights." Yury lifted Georgyi, who stepped into his boost, and caught the first big branch. "I'm glad I grabbed these pants," he grunted. "This tree is sharp to climb."

Georgyi had climbed only five meters up the tree before the remaining three foot sphere hovered above him. Georgyi tightly griped at tree branches, but needle-like rays of light inflamed his skin once more. He screamed in pain and covered his eyes. Branches snapped as Georgyi's fall tore them loose. Snow and broken tree limbs avalanched toward the crowd below, accelerated by his weight, and an immense pressing-down force emanating from the sphere.

The deluge of matter, light, force, and Georgyi's body weight struck Yury full on. As clouds of snowy branches settled, two bodies lay silent below the tree. The sweat of climbing turned to frost on Georgyi's skin. Neither of the bodies continued to shiver.

"Quickly," Dyatlov screamed, "run away!" Everyone ran from the sphere and from the smothered fire. Dyatlov, Zina, and Rustem headed in the direction of the tent.

"I'm just too cold to walk any further," Zina cried. "Let me rest here a moment."

"No, we need shelter." Rustem dragged Zina with one arm. Dyatlov took her other.

"We can't stop here," Dyatlov said. "Hypothermia settles in. We have to get warmed up. Keep moving!"

Suddenly, a twenty-four foot sphere hovered overhead. Another searing light beam flashed down on the three. Slobodin was hit head on with the bolt. It fractured his skull from the inside out. Dyatlov released Zina and collapsed onto the snow 300 meters from the pine tree. Rustern dragged Zina, but dropped her 480 meters from the pine. His head throbbing, at 630 meters from the tree he dropped lifelessly into the snow. Both spheres zipped out of sight.

Survivors 1959

Nicolas, Lyudmila, Alex, and Alexander had come back to the pine tree. Georgyi and Yury lay deadly silent beneath.

"You need these no more, my brother," Alexander Zolotaryov said as he pulled the pants off Georgyi. "I need to survive this."

"That ravine might lead to some shelter," Nicolas pointed. He'd scanned 75 meters away with his blurred vision. "It might have ice like a stream valley. At least, it's further into the woods."

"Maybe these things won't notice us deeper into that valley," Alex voiced hope. "But, we have to make another fire."

"I still have a couple of matches in my coat," Lyudmila said, as they stumbled through the snow shivering. "Can you see again, Nicolas?" Lyudmila panted.

"Only a little. It's still fuzzy." Nicolas pushed through the drifts.

The group struggled silently through brush in the bottom of the ravine until Lyudmila screamed and fell. "What is it? Are you all right?" Alexander and Alex rushed to help her up.

Writer's Bloc III

"I stepped in a hole, I stabbed my foot on a branch, I'm terrified, I'm freezing, I'm cut, and all our other friends are dead. Of course, I'm not all right!" she screamed.

"Look, let's hope they won't find us here," Nicholas said. Alexander tore off a piece of Georgyi's pants to wrap up Lyudmila's foot.

Suddenly, the largest metallic-orange sphere hovered overhead. A lightning bolt-like probe bathed them in light. They tried to stand, to move away, or to run. Lyudmila fell to the snow in a seizure. Writhing in pain from the razor points of light, she bit off her own tongue. Then, beneath fractured ribs, her heart stopped, and she lay still.

The sphere's probing radiation over-charged the hollow space inside their bones. Ribs split open from the inside out, broken like popping balloons. Then, as energy probed deeper into their chests, it arrested beating and stopped their hearts.

Nicolas took the hardest blow. The bones of his skull crackled from inside as his brain was probed. All four collapsed in the snow. The sphere zipped away.

Slowly, Alexander Zolotaryov stood to shake himself. He felt his ribs burning when he breathed. Somehow, his heart had weathered the jolt. In excruciating pain, he stooped to gather the coat and hat from Lyudmila's body.

"Sorry, my dear. Maybe one of us can live through this." Alexander assessed his situation through grisly soldier's humor. "Even though the clothes are really not my style." With these last remaining companions dead, returning to the tent was his only chance if he expected to survive. Desperation drove him to leave the ravine.

The sphere returned. Only a moment passed before one last bolt of light struck his broken ribs. Like a bomb inside his chest, it fatally stopped his heart. With one last sigh, Alexander's body went limp and dropped. Snow whirlwinded from trees and sides of the small valley as the sphere lifted.

The four now slept in silence, tucked under a thick blanket of white.

The spheres, noting the frailty of these "vessels of life," gathered their compelling unknown force and vanished toward the horizon.

Late Night Visitor

Yuri Yudin awoke suddenly to intense bright orange, burning light. Rays of ultra-violet indigo sparked out like sharp pointed razors of ice from a three foot orb. It's suspended proximity hovered close and microwaved fire-pain through every cell of his body.

Yuri struggled to wake, to move, to rise up against the light's strength. His exhausted resistance finally succumbed to the weight of its energy deluge. Yuri collapsed back under the energy flood tide, drowned in radiation. Light too intense to resist smashed him back. Fluid gravity force pressed down like flood waters from a bursting dam. His flesh burned from the inside out. Every nerve cell cried out, yet, Yuri Yudin did not. Time slowed into a slow-motion eternity. Yuri felt his face burning and sharp stabbing needles of force crackling his already grey hair.

"*You have finally come back for me,*" his mind slurred. Pain surges mounted inside as skull and chest bones fractured. Amidst the searing light-pain, his body expired. Yuri smiled as he sighed out his last breath. Tears of joy rolled from blinded eyes, then down his sunburned cheeks. Closed eyes clouded like a wild bird's held too close to a candle.

In the Morning

Stewart knocked at the door to thank Yuri, but no noise greeted him. "Yuri?" Stewart spoke loudly, in case the old man was sleeping. The forceful knocking had loosened the latch. The attic room door swung slowly open.

A strange feeling filled the room. *It smells like an electric motor burned out*, Stewart thought. In a moment, he knew.

Yuri Yudin was dead. His ruddy, sunburned complexion and Yuri's vibrant gray hair flashed Stewart instantly back to Dyatlov Pass descriptions.

Then, his attention was caught by the old tent zipper stretched atop the blankets. It felt warm to his touch. With a cautious hand, he touched Yuri's cheek. *The body is cold,* Stewart determined. *But somehow, this all makes sense.*

The Witness

Stewart returned to the room as medical officials collected the body. "Do you need me to sign papers, or anything?" Stewart asked.

"No, the report's completed. He has no family. The State will handle it." The official turned to Stewart. "Do you want this?"

Stewart took the old zipper offered. Grasping the top, he pulled it down about six inches and zipped it back. It was cool. "Yes, thanks. It'll remind me of Yuri."

"I'm glad it means something to somebody." The two medical men rolled the body out of the bedroom.

Stewart carefully replaced the zipper in its jar. He was mysteriously drawn to the window. He spoke as he looked out to the mountain, "Now, you've finally joined your friends, old man. Rest in peace."

Flamingo Wash
Carol Deanna

Shortly after ten o'clock on a mild October evening in Sin City, Janey Taft dropped her oversized backpack behind a concrete block wall bordering the Flamingo Wash.

The wash greeted her with a moody breeze that sifted through her short, layered brown hair, grazed her bare arms, and rattled the tall stalks of reed grasses that grew along the ragged edges of the murmuring stream. Anxiety fluttered in her stomach.

As if on cue, her cell phone vibrated. She answered the phone without looking at the display. "Hi, Belle."

For almost a year Janey's uneasy alliance with Belle Chandler had ruled her life. Tonight she would finally get the upper hand. But not yet.

"Where are you?"

"I'm at Site 10." Janey stared into the night as she spoke. The lights of the casinos and hotels on the Strip, less than a mile away, blotted out the stars. "The time is…" she glanced at her watch, "10:27 and I'll be moving on to Site 11 at 10:45."

"I know what time it is. I wanted to make sure you were on schedule. Harry will meet you at Site 11. He needs a bag of Premium."

Writer's Bloc III

"But I thought—"

"I'll meet you at Site 12, just as we planned. Is that clear?"

"Absolutely, but…"

Belle disconnected, cutting Janey off.

Patience, she reminded herself, pulling her penlight off her belt, where it was clipped next to a canister of pepper spray and her cell phone. With the end so near, she couldn't afford to deviate from her normal routine.

After shining her light into the shrubbery along the wall to check for roaches, spiders, ants, toads or any other lurkers, she pulled out a few dishes hidden behind the bushy growth. When she unzipped her backpack, cats approached from all directions, illuminated by the security lights of the businesses backing both sides of the wash. One scruffy cat with tattered ears crossed the wash below from the other side, jumping from rock to rock to avoid the steady flow of shallow water.

Janey had been involved with animal rescue groups for ten years in Minneapolis until, forty-five years old and newly divorced, she'd moved to Las Vegas a year ago. This was her first experience with feral cat colonies.

"Hi, guys." She poured food into three large heavy-duty plastic bowls. "Aren't you a good-looking crew! Are you hungry tonight?" Pushing the bowls back into the space between the wall and the shrubbery, she kept up a mindless chatter while her mind cycled through an endless loop—had she laid all the groundwork? Had she planned for every contingency?

Forcing herself back to the task at hand, she wrote down the number of cats—nine present, one tiger striped cat missing—in a notebook she carried in her back pocket.

After jotting down a few more observations, she pulled a plastic garbage bag out of her backpack. While she policed the site, she mentally prepared herself for the next stop on her route. Situated close to the Flamingo Wash, but not on it, Site 11 sat behind an abandoned nightclub, separated from an apartment complex by a six-foot chain link fence.

Three nights earlier, she and Belle had gone to Site 11 together. Engrossed in counting heads—at least thirteen cats drifted in and out of the shadowy recesses of the building—Janey started when she heard a tremendous THWACK. The chain link fence clattered and shook as if a desert wind had slammed into it. Belle shrieked, and Janey whirled to face a security guard wielding a baton on the other side of the fence.

"You people are trashing this place. Those hairballs hang around the dumpsters over here, and there's empty cat food tins all over the parking lot. The manager is pissed, and if you don't keep those vandals out of here, they're dog food."

This was not their first confrontation. Brock had been dictatorial, but friendly, when they first met. When they hadn't responded to his overtures, he had resorted to outright harassment. In his late twenties, tall and wiry, he had a diagonal scar through his left eyebrow that gave him a menacing appearance, and he usually relied on verbal abuse to make his point.

Belle, fearless and formidable, stepped up to the fence.

"First of all," said Belle, "this is a registered feral cat colony. Second, we do not give the cats soft food in tin cans. Your tenants must be putting out food, and they are the ones you should talk to."

THWACK. The fence jangled again. "You think I'm stupid? There's more going on here than a cat colony. Get those cats out of here and take your so-called volunteers with you. If you don't take care of the problem, we will! Get it?"

"If any of those cats, even one of those cats, is harmed or disappears, I'll have you up on charges of cruelty to animals.

And that's a serious charge here in Nevada. Get it?"

"Oooh, I'm scared, now." Brock smirked and twirled his baton. "You need evidence to file charges."

Belle had a death grip on the fence, but she spoke with a controlled confidence. "Not a problem. You've been making threats against these cats, and we have a witness." She glanced over at Janey, standing a few feet away. Belle had a temper, and her face was stiff with outrage.

THWACK. "This is your last warning. Get those filthy animals out of here."

"Yeah, and you know where you can stick that baton, you bobble-headed, scum-sucking dirtbag."

"Bitch!" THWACK. The fence shimmied.

Janey put her hand on her pepper spray.

THWACK. The fence listed toward Belle, forcing her to step back. "Keep those hairballs off our property." With that parting shot, their would-be intimidator had stalked away.

Only a few hours later, on the same night, Belle had called Janey to tell her, in a taut voice, that her husband's sister had been killed in a one-car accident. "Janey," she had said, "I'm counting on you to run the store for a few days."

Since then, Janey had been busy with The Lynx Connection, Belle's cat care store. She hadn't gone back to Site 11, since other volunteers had been available.

Closing her garbage bag, Janey decided that Brock might be a complication, but she wouldn't know how to deal with him until she knew what the situation was.

Twenty minutes later she parked her SUV outside the fenced enclosure of the defunct Serpent's Tooth jazz club. Making as little noise as possible, she exited the car, retrieving her backpack and a five-pound bag of Premium Lynx Mix cat food from the luggage compartment.

Belle sold her own brand of cat food, called Lynx Mix. The Lynx Connection was also the headquarters for her cat rescue organization, LYNX (Connecting with our feline friends through our Trap, Neuter, Release program).

Janey eased her way in between two sections of the fence. As she put out food for the cats in the only area that had vegetation—a few palm trees set in a tangle of overgrowth—she turned her attention to the fence a dozen yards away.

In contrast to the abandoned property, the parking lot of the Fairhaven Villas next door was well lit. When a security guard putt-putted by on an electric cart, Janey, on her knees in front of the food bowls, remained still. Two of the cats chose that moment to engage each other, and an unearthly screeching and howling ensued.

The electric cart stopped, the driver peered through the fence, and Janey threw her backpack at the two snarling combatants. One took off, and the other sat and started washing his face.

"Hi, there." The security guard, an older man who in no way resembled Brock, approached the fence. He was a retired New York City cop who worked part-time.

Janey rose and brushed twigs and grass off her jeans. "Hey, Harry." She picked up the extra bag of cat food and met him at the fence. "We have a new cat, an intact Tommy who shows up once or twice a week to bully the cats. If we can catch him, we'll get him neutered."

Harry nodded and pulled a section of the fence toward him, creating a gap. "It's hard to catch him if he doesn't have a pattern of behavior. A random predator can outwit law enforcement for years."

Janey handed over the Premium Lynx Mix cat food to Harry. No one, she thought, suppressing the inner qualms that quickened her heartbeat and threatened to close her throat, would suspect that the bag contained a shrink-wrapped package of cocaine.

Their transaction completed, Harry relaxed into the posture of a man ready for a gossip session. In what she hoped was a conversational tone, Janey said, "Where's Brock? Did he change his days off?"

"Brock is..." Harry hesitated and scratched his nose. "Brock was found over in the wash this morning. Someone worked him over pretty good." He pressed his lips together. "They took him over to Desert Springs Hospital, but he didn't make it."

Janey's mouth opened and closed, and the image of a man entered her mind. Belle's half-brother, Al—huge, heavily tattooed, a man of few words, and completely devoted to Belle.

"It looks like the perp used his own baton on him. Tossed it on top of him when he was through. Are you all right?" Janey's lack of response finally registered with him.

She has no limits, Janey thought, horrified. She managed to speak, but her voice cracked. "Brock had an attitude. I didn't like him, but I wouldn't have wished that on him."

"He didn't make many friends, and I guess he used that baton once too often. He applied to the Police Academy, you know, and they wouldn't take him. He was a borderline...oh, hell, he's gone now. What difference does it make?"

Shaken, Janey finished her duties at Site 11 as quickly as possible. Panic coiled in her stomach, and she swallowed repeatedly to suppress the urge to vomit.

She drove to Site 12 on automatic pilot, her thoughts entering a maze of speculation, what ifs, and possibilities. Driving east on Flamingo Road, she crossed the Strip, oblivious of the monoliths—Caesars Palace, the Bellagio, Bill's and Bally's—anchoring the intersection.

When she had ventured into The Lynx Connection for the first time, shortly after she arrived in Las Vegas, she knew at once that she was in the presence of a charismatic personality. A vibrant redhead in her mid-thirties, Belle exuded sensuality with her graceful posture and provocative clothing. But it was her salesmanship that won Janey over. She left with several bags of food, vitamin supplements, toys and accessories for her aging cat.

After a few more visits, Janey agreed to volunteer as a caretaker for Belle's feral cat colonies. She had a pension from her twenty-plus years working for the city of Minneapolis that covered her basic living expenses.

A couple of friends who had moved to Vegas from Minneapolis had assured her that, with her background, she could easily get a job with the city. Unfortunately, a hiring freeze put the job she had expected on hold. As time went on, she started working in the store a few afternoons a week, and Belle paid her at a rate slightly higher than minimum wage.

At what point, Janey wondered, could she have backed out? Belle gave her a small raise after three months, along with more hours and more responsibility. She learned to process orders and found that Belle provided a thriving delivery service to residents throughout the Vegas Valley.

Al drove to Los Angeles every Sunday, returning Monday with a shipment of Lynx Mix cat food. Tuesday through Friday he left early every morning with a loaded van, some days driving as far as Pahrump and Indian Springs, where Belle had contracts with a couple of smaller stores.

LYNX was the best funded and most well organized animal rescue group Janey had ever worked with, and she supposed the income from the store and the cat food sales was partly responsible. Belle mentioned that she had a few large donors, as well, but she kept her own books and the finances of her business were a closely guarded secret.

As Janey approached Site 12, she thought about the structure of LYNX. The organization paid for food and water, dishes, backpacks, cell phones, traps, and any veterinary expenses involved in supporting fifteen feral cat colonies. Belle scheduled eight volunteers, including Janey, to manage the sites on a rotating schedule.

Parking behind a professional building near the Flamingo Wash, Janey pulled on a windbreaker, leaving it open, over her T-shirt. She checked her surroundings before gathering her supplies, including a trap, and headed to Site 12.

A high wooden fence lined the back of the parking lot. Janey removed three or four slats and slipped through. Tension rippled through her as she inspected the terrain on the other side, and she shivered when a chilly current of air brushed past.

Along this stretch of the wash, foliage grew in abundance, anchoring the banks and extending into the meandering stream. Moonlight filtered through the ferny branches of tamarisk trees, reflecting off the water that trickled through a dense cover of shrubs, bushes and reeds. Across the gully lights twinkled here and there in an upscale gated community.

"Ready or not, " she said, shoring herself up for the confrontation ahead. "Here I am." The piquant scent of damp vegetation filled her nostrils from the ravine below as she regained her sense of purpose.

She strode over to a level patch of ground several feet from the south bank, the gravelly soil crunching under her boots.

"Calypso. Here, kitty. Calypso." She took a bag of food out of her backpack, and five cats materialized out of the shadows when the dry food rattled into the bowls. Calypso, a tawny long-haired cat, his gold eyes glowing in the dark, lay in wait nearby, too wary to come closer.

Janey knew the name of her target cat, because she had found his breakaway collar one night hanging from the branch of a hardy shrub. He was, in all likelihood, a foreclosure cat, abandoned by accident or design. If her plans worked out tonight, and they would, she reassured herself, she would adopt Calypso.

Pretending she didn't see him, Janey walked past him

with the trap and made a little production out of placing it in the shelter of a nearby bush. She opened a can of soft food, the only situation in which she deviated from the dry food policy, arranged it in a little dish inside the trap and put the can in a garbage bag for disposal later.

After she made her notebook entries, she spread a towel on the ground and sat, leaning against a tree as a backrest with her backpack as a buffer. As soon as she settled into a comfortable position, her cell phone vibrated, and she took a deep breath.

"Hi, Belle."

"Where are you?" Belle spoke over a murmur of voices in the background.

"Site 12. I fed the cats and set up a trap for Calypso." She looked out over the chasm of the wash, acutely aware of her isolation in this secluded area.

"Everyone came back here after the viewing," said Belle, irritation spiking in her voice.

"How long…" Janey began.

"Belle, where is that Hawaiian vacation album?" A sonorous male voice on the other end of the line overrode the rest of her question.

"Stay put," said Belle, terminating the call.

In the stillness of the wash, cool currents of air wafted through and the moon played hide and seek with the gathering clouds. Like Belle, Janey thought. Alternately incandescent and elusive.

She fingered the LYNX logo pin she wore on the left side of her T-Shirt. Belle had given it to her along with a promotion and a serious raise a few months earlier. Its ornate green and gold stylization of a bobcat ready to spring clashed with Janey's tastes and practical nature, but it seemed appropriate for tonight's outing.

Her promotion had come about after a long, exhausting day

at the shop. Janey and Belle closed the store together at 9:00 p.m. Over pizza and diet sodas, Janey told Belle that she was looking for another job. "I have an interview with the county next week. I would rather work here, but I need to earn more money."

When Belle didn't respond, she went on, "My pension doesn't stretch as far as I hoped. I have two kids in college, credit card debt that my ex-husband ran up when we were married, and my ten-year-old car needs major repairs."

Belle toyed with her pizza, her well-shaped brows drawn together, her lips pursed. Janey finished her soda, and sat back, giving Belle time to review her options. When Belle slapped her hand down on the table, Janey straightened.

"You can make more money working for me, but first you must promise me that this conversation stays between us. Whatever you decide."

Janey waited a few moments before she said, "Okay."

"I provide a courier service for a powerful organization. If you're willing to deliver an unspecified product from Point A to Point B, I can guarantee you a large fee for each transaction."

Maintaining eye contact with Belle, Janey summoned every bit of resolve she had, and asked, "Are you talking about drugs?"

"Does it make a difference?" Belle's gaze didn't waver.

"Yes." Street drugs were abhorrent to Janey, but she needed the job. "If we're talking Mary Kaye products, there's no risk, no problem. If it's drugs, I want to know what I'm getting into."

Belle shrugged and a tiny smile tugged at the corners of her mouth. "We transport packages and we're well paid to do so. Our client manufactures a product for an affluent segment of society, people who can afford to pay top dollar. Our role is to deliver the product to a designated distributor. We are nothing more than a conduit."

When Janey hesitated, Belle said, "There's no cash involved. We're on a monthly retainer."

Translation, thought Janey, LYNX is laundering money for a drug cartel.

In the end, she agreed, with some trepidation, to be a courier. A percentage of the Lynx Mix cat food bags, labeled Premium, contained the packaged cocaine. At each feral cat colony, a contact had been established, someone who would normally be in the area, such as Harry, in his job as a part-time security guard.

Janey left the store each night with two or three Premium Lynx Mix bags, which she threw in the back of her SUV along with bags of cat litter and other innocuous clutter. She had a schedule, visiting all the sites in rotation, but in a different order and at different times each week.

If she were caught, Janey realized, Belle could claim that Janey acted on her own. Somehow, Janey had to shift the balance of power in their relationship. The opportunity had presented itself that morning, when Belle had dashed into the store, dressed in a conservative black pantsuit, her wild mane of hair pulled back from her face into an elegant twist.

"I'm on my way to the airport," she told Janey. "Geoff's brother and his wife are coming in from Chicago, and I've been delegated to meet them." After glancing around to make sure no one was within earshot, she lowered her voice. "An important client has a special shipment he wants delivered, but time is of the essence. Al went out of town this morning, and I have to play the devoted spouse this week." She grimaced. "Meredith should never have been let out of rehab. At least she didn't kill anyone else, but her timing really sucks."

"What can I do to help?" said Janey, ignoring Belle's callous reference to her sister-in-law's death."

"Someone will pass me the package at the viewing. Be at

Writer's Bloc III

Site 12 by 11:30 tonight. Since we live so close, I'll be able to slip away and meet you there. I'll hand the package off to you and you can deliver it."

Janey stretched, listening for a footstep, a cough, any indication of another presence. Where was Belle? It was almost midnight.

SNAP! Janey, startled out of her musings, knew instantly what had happened. She jumped up, grabbed the towel and ran over to the cage. Calypso yowled, a mournful wail that rose up over the wash as he thrashed from side to side in the steel mesh enclosure. Janey threw the towel over the cage. After a feeble protest, he fell silent, and the incessant chatter of myriad insects resumed. "You're a good boy," Janey told him. "You're safe now. You're going to be just fine."

While her adrenaline rush subsided, Janey paced the bank of the wash, pleased that she'd caught Calypso, restless as she waited for Belle. From time to time, she glanced over to the opposite bank and the housing development beyond it.

When Belle appeared at last, she walked into view from the northeast, where the wash curved out of sight. She crossed over at a spot where the channel narrowed, supple and sure-footed as she stepped from boulder to boulder.

Janey met her at the top of the bank.

Skipping the preliminaries, Belle said, "I have to get back right away. Take this to the Vegas Valley Veterinary Clinic on Boulder Highway." Reciting specific directions, she pulled off her knapsack and held it up by the strap on top. "Give this to the night attendant, a woman named Martha." She pulled at a tab on the bottom of the bag, revealing a clear plastic package containing a white powder, nestled in a secret compartment.

"Okay," said Janey into her modified LYNX logo pin. "Let's do it." She pulled a badge out of her pocket and held it up in the moonlight. "Metro Police, you're under arrest."

Lights sprang up all over the wash, advancing toward them amid a chorus of "Metro Police" and "Freeze."

Janey had expected Belle's attack. She feinted to the left, but when Belle pulled her off-balance, they both rolled down the bank. After a brief struggle, which left them both sopping wet and bruised from their contact with the rocks in the bed of the wash, Janey gained the upper hand. In a few practiced moves, she forced Belle to her knees and cuffed her hands behind her back.

After they brought Belle up out of the wash and read her her rights, two officers, one of them female, took Belle out to an unmarked car for the ride to the station.

Dave, one of the two remaining plainclothes cops, slapped Janey on the back. "Way to go, J.T. You're the best. Aren't you glad we talked you into moving to Vegas?"

"Yeah, yeah. You promised me a slot in Homicide, and I ended up with this freaking undercover job."

"And see how well that worked out. You bagged Judge Chandler's wife. From the information you've given us, she's the key to breaking up a whole network," said Dave, her friend and former partner from the Minneapolis Police Department. "By the way, that Homicide slot is still open. I heard you're at the top of the list."

After a little more good-natured sparring, Janey told the guys to go on ahead.

"I'll be up as soon as I clear the site."

Alone in the Flamingo Wash, she savored her triumph. The moon emerged from behind a cloud and a gentle breeze stirred with a sigh of relief. In the back of her mind, Janey heard a decisive SNAP.

She laughed, picked up her trap and walked out.

A MINI LOVE STORY
Sid Goodman

"Hey Pops!" they shouted in unison. "Can we get a hot dog and drink at the refreshment stand?" Bedraggled hair dripped salt water on the beach towel and sand grit encapsulated their feet. "Sure, but dry off first," he cautioned as he retrieved a ten-dollar bill from his wallet. "And don't forget the change," he reminded his three exuberant offspring as they dashed off.

His responsibilities as sole custodial parent had dominated the better part of his life since their mother had left some ten years earlier. He enjoyed those days when he could indulge his charges instead of acting like a benevolent dictator over them.

How segmented each week has become, he mused while watching them play and act silly in the wavy water. *Kid care, house care, two jobs and writing a damn text book—I never seem to have any fun time for myself. Dating takes so much work and time. How many weekends have I gone out with someone only to wish I'd spent those wasted hours planning meals, preparing school lunches, watching TV travel programs or just reading a good book —stuff like that?* Longer term involvements didn't give him any satisfaction either. *Nuts to relationships, who needs them? My motto shall be "Never Again!"*

Late Friday afternoon, after the weekly status meeting in the manager's office, everyone was eager to head home for a relaxing weekend. One of the group leaders hung back as the rest of the staff filed out of the office.

"This may sound somewhat forward," she began, as she closed the door, "but ah wonder if ah could ask a personal favor?" She spoke with a soft Southern accent, reflective of her North Carolina origins.

"Sure," the boss replied robotically, more interested in tidying up his desk and getting his own butt on the road. He'd promised the kids Japanese takeout for dinner that night. "What do you need?"

"Well, ah invited my older sistah and her two teenage daughtahs to come to California. Ah'm trying to soften the grief and mourning they are experiencing since the unexpected loss this year of their husband and father. Ah think she needs to have contact with some adults other than me," she explained, and then continued her preamble. "Ah've told her a lot about you and thought perhaps you'd like to stop by the house for coffee and a brief introduction. Ah know she'd be thrilled to meet you."

Pulling off his glasses and putting one temple in his mouth, he thought, *I don't think I like where this is going. I hope this isn't a matchmaking exercise.*

"Please bring your kids. This will give mah nieces a chance to meet some kids their own age as well," she added.

Succumbing to the somewhat desperate tone of her request, he conceded that it would not be that inconvenient and might turn out to be an interesting experience for the kids as well.

"Okay, I guess we can do this. I have to get my oldest daughter off to school this coming Sunday and since you live close to the airport. I'll ask the twins to come with and we'll stop by afterwards. Would that suit?"

"Oh yes," she answered, "that would be perfect."

Sunday arrived and he loaded his three kids into the car. "We'll drop your sister at the American terminal," he explained to the twins. "After that, I want you to meet some kids whose dad died recently. Their mom also wants to meet us."

Traffic from the airport was light, so he arrived at the apartment a few minutes early. His group leader had taken her nieces to pick up some goodies at the grocery store. Taken by surprise, Older Sister greeted Younger Sister's "boss" by nervously lapsing into a stereotypical, heavily-accented, rapid-fire monologue suggestive of Jean Smart on *Designing Women.*

"Why don't you sit heah in the kitchen?—No not that chair, sit over theah so I can talk to your face—Did you get your daughtah off to school alright?—So these are your twins—Can I get y'all something to drink?—Perhaps the two of y'all would be more comfortable if y'all go watch TV in the living room and then your daddy could move over to a cooler place by the window."

It scared the bejeezuz out of him. *Good grief*, he thought, *what have I gotten myself into?*

Upon their return the nieces were introduced to the twins and the four preteens went outside to check each other out and hang. The three adults adjourned to the living room with coffee and cookies. He noticed that Older Sister calmed down, slowing her speech, and slouched ever so slightly on the couch. She spoke clearly and intelligently about the unexpected turn of events that brought her to this time and place.

"Mah husband, an Air Force reserve officer, was called for special weekend duty," she explained. "He was in Intelligence, so the purpose of the trip was very hush-hush." She straightened from her slouch, and clasping her hands on her knees, bent forward in his direction and sighed wearily. "Next thing ah know, the Air Force advised me of his sudden death. It took days before they brought him home."

He leaned closer to better hear her. The cadence of her Southern drawl faded and she spoke with less intensity but more emotion than in the kitchen.

Now there's a classy lady, he thought, *certainly a lot more intriguing than some of the women I've dated lately. Definitely beats the Parents Without Partners crowd. On the other hand, her sister works for me and, considering the proximity of her husband's death, I think it would be most impolitic and ungracious of me to pursue anything beyond an acquaintanceship.*

Two weeks later, after the regular Friday afternoon reviews, the group leader hung back once again.

"Well, what do you think about mah older sistah?" she asked.

"Frankly," he answered, "she's quite the lady. I was most enchanted by her Southern grace and charm."

"Ah'm glad you think so. She's getting a little cabin fever, and truth be told, ah just don't have time to chauffer her and the girls for round-the-clock entertainment. She loves to shop but ah don't have the stamina and ah'm not rich enough to keep up with her—"

"So what is it you think I can do?" he interrupted.

"Honestly, it would so be a big help if you would take her out one night, maybe just for dinner and a little conversation." Her cheeks and brow flushed from having asked the favor. "Ah'll even pay," she added quickly.

He leaned back in his executive chair and chewed his pen, alternatively staring at his loyal colleague and then the ceiling, mentally debating the implications of the request. He had concluded that any socializing with Older Sister would be inappropriate. This request, however, appeared to nullify any impropriety resulting from dating one's subordinate's sister. Besides, the favor seemed benign enough and might, in fact, be fun.

"Okay, I'll be glad to take her to dinner. And forget about your paying, my ego won't allow that and my budget can handle it. I have your home number, so I'll call as soon as I figure out what to do with my kids."

For this first date, she wore a pastel-hued diaphanous dress with a matching shawl that contrasted with the gilt and brightly colored décor of the Indian restaurant. A tape of raga provided grating, faux-exotica music in the dining area. The table held the remnants of the eclectic South Asian food he had ordered, more to impress her than to satisfy their evening hunger.

As they sipped tea from delicate cups with hand painted blue periwinkles, he listened intently to her Southern drawl as she described her life since her husband died. The shawl would edge slowly off her right shoulder as she talked, exposing a smooth pink-white skin that distracted his concentration. The woman exhibited a gracefulness consistent with Southern Belle gentility, yet a sensual aura that contradicted a prim and proper stereotype.

The conversation never seemed to pale, despite the impatient intrusions by the waiter signifying a desire for the two diners to finish and leave. Older Sister did not appear nervous, yet he detected some reticence when she asked about his life as a single parent. Perhaps she thought she might be prying too much. He explained why he chose, actually insisted on, full - rather than shared custody of his children, the mistakes he made, the extraordinary time demands required, and the lack of any significant social life.

He described his growing discomfort of relationships with women, especially after the rise of feminism that led to the departure of the kids' mother and his subsequent divorce. Despite his desire to be a charming and focused host, he feared that he came across pedantic and officious.

Trying not to sound pompous, he passed on little

anecdotal events that illustrated how he came to understand that single-parenting is doable and rewarding as well, sort of a mini pep talk.

He told her how he always kept a book in his car while waiting for his kids to perform in a school play or musicale. "That way," he explained, "I was always there for them, seen by their friends and teachers as being an interested parent. But when nothing was going on, I could go back to the car and catch up on my reading. When my son would race cross-country, I could catch a brief nap until it was time to cheer him on at the finish line."

He laughed at the memory and added, "Heck, one year I even ran in a 5K race with the twins. They ran the 10K part and passed me halfway through."

Throughout the meal and conversation, he noticed her studying him, rarely diverting her eyes, as if everything he said was deep and erudite. He tried hard not to be flattered. *Now if only she'd keep that damn shawl on her shoulder!*

When they finally left the restaurant, he suggested a nightcap at a rooftop bar with a magnificent view of the bay. She hesitated, "Ahr you sure you don't need to be home with your kids?"

"They're at their grandmother's for the weekend. Why? Are you beginning to worry about your two?"

"No, they went to a movie and pizza with Awntie; she'll get them to bed on time."

Huge plate glass windows revealed twinkling lights from the southern peninsula competing with those from the stars in the cloudless sky. The gentle strumming of a guitar provided a romantic backdrop in the bar, which they shared with only three other couples. Candles on the tables cast tiny galaxies of soft yellow-orange light. He loosened his tie, wondering whether she'd find the act too informal or out of place for a first encounter. They continued talking, now about his love of travel. He told her of some of the places he'd been —Mexico, Fiji, Israel, and Cyprus, and how much he looked forward to visiting new and intriguing destinations once the kids were on their own.

"Ah've never traveled much except to South Carolina, New Jersey and California," she said with a touch of regret. "Oh, mah husband, mah sister and ah did take a quick trip to Tijuana once."

"Did you enjoy that?" he asked.

"Ah guess so. Ah just never thought about what it's like to travel to really faraway places. Ah wouldn't know wheah to go or what to see."

"Well let me tell you the best part," he said as he removed his glasses and rubbed the bridge of his nose. "Ten percent is saying 'Oh I've been there' while watching a travelogue on TV or one-upping some snob at a cocktail party. Another ten percent is remembering the anecdotes and unplanned events while sitting in front of a fire with snifters of brandy. But eighty percent of the fun is having someone with you to share your ooh ahs."

They sipped their drinks and took in the view until closing time. Wishing that the moment not end, he reluctantly paid the bill. They went down the elevator in silence and when they stepped out onto the sidewalk, he removed his jacket and put it around her shoulders to ward off the early morning sea mist. She casually put her arm into the crook of his elbow, causing him to shudder from the touch as he escorted her to the car.

No longer her sister's boss, but her gentleman caller, he parked the car in the driveway next to the stairs leading up to the apartment. With the motor still running, they exchanged the compulsory *I had a really nice time, thank you*, neither one moving to get out of the car. He looked into her eyes, then at her dress with the shawl now completely fallen off her shoulder. He put his arm around her and drew her closer for a goodnight kiss. She obliged by tilting her head just so and moved to shorten the distance between their lips.

The kiss lasted forever infusing sensations that coursed through his body, axons and neurons bombarding the pleasure sensors in his brain. He wanted to convert the moment into a seduction, but his conscience prevented him from doing so. *One More Time*, he thought and then applied a little more pressure on her lips.

When they finally came up for air, he uttered the only sound he could—WOW!

Twenty-five years have passed since he changed his motto from *Never Again* to *One More Time*. He's lost count of the foreign cities and countries he and Older Sister have visited. All five kids are successfully on their own, engaged in eclectic adventures with their families and friends.

Time has erased the bitterness he had when they first met. They live in a comfort zone of love, trust, and happiness ---WOW!

Petty Theft
Carrie Ann Lahain

They caught him in the parking lot. A skinny female security guard and two bulky stock boys with pimples.

"What do you want?" Julius asked, backing up against a minivan.

The stock boys closed in, stopping just short of actually touching him. The security officer, a big-haired broad, stood back with her hand on her radio. "Sir, you're going to have to come with me." She lowered her voice. "You were seen, sir. At the deli counter."

"No use denying it." The fatter of the two stock boys grabbed Julius' carrier bag. "We got cameras."

"And I got a receipt." Julius pulled a crumpled strip of paper out of his jacket pocket. It was all there. A loaf of bread. Brown mustard. Half a pound of rice pudding.

"Would you take off your jacket, sir?"

"I'm not taking off nothing." Panicking, Julius flattened himself against the car. "You call the police."

It wasn't the smartest demand Julius had ever made, but he figured that Cruella and her high school drop-out cronies wouldn't really want a senior citizen arrested in front of their store. He was wrong. The police arrived five minutes later, and six minutes later they had relieved Julius of his jacket and the pound of extra-thin-sliced premium Genoa salami wedged up his left sleeve.

Writer's Bloc III

Julius Bach was not a poor man, exactly. He and his wife owned a house in a decent neighborhood. They had his pension from the post office. Maura's disability check covered half the mortgage and most of her medications. The few dollars left over she invested at the only casino located within the battery-charge distance of her motorized wheelchair. Still, if there was one thing Julius had learned in the four years since they had retired to Las Vegas, it was that everyone you met was out for what he could get. And everyone seemed to be getting something except Julius who, if he had known what a hole this town was, would not have bothered leaving Brooklyn.

It was Maura's fault.

God, if he could live life over again. Julius wasn't the marrying kind. He'd known this, but he'd gone and done it anyway. He'd met Maura at a karaoke bar in Brooklyn Heights. She sang *Where the Boys Are*. Her voice was okay, but that she actually looked a lot like Connie Francis—dark and winsome—was what really got his attention. They got married during a trip to Vegas the next year. Then, when his dad left him a few bucks, they bought a vacation place there. They figured they'd rent it out until they retired.

Things were going great until Maura's fingers started to tingle. Julius would always remember that day. It was the day Maura found Barbara Tannenbaum's *Television Times* in their bedroom.

"Who the hell is Barbara Tannenbaum?" she had asked, slinging the chunky magazine with its damning address label across the room at him. It missed, landing on the windowsill. Julius didn't like people throwing things at him and told her so, though his threat to retaliate didn't go over well. "Just you try it. I'll have the police chain you to a wall."

Maura couldn't do this, Julius knew, even if she did

handle payroll for the New York City Police Department. But she could make his life miserable. And she would.

"This is nuts," he said, cringing as she grabbed for a pair of scissors and cut his uniform belt in half. "The woman in 6A is in Florida for three weeks. What does she need with the *Television Times?*"

"Are you doing that again?" Maura threw aside the destroyed belt. "You're supposed to put mail in people's boxes, not take it out."

"She doesn't need it." And it was a buck fifty down at the corner store.

"You're gonna lose your pension." She sank onto the bed and pried off her pumps. "End up in Federal prison. Would you like that, Julius?" Grimacing, she started massaging the fingers of her left hand. "The stealing has got to stop."

What stealing? So he pocketed unwanted television listings here and there. Maybe a pack of gum or bottle of aspirin. The stores weren't out to do him any favors. And his job? If not for his damn pension, he would have quit years ago.

By the end of the week, his job took second place to a larger problem. Maura's tingling fingers started to burn. She could barely hold a fork, much less enter police payroll information into a computer for eight hours a day.

Within a week they knew. Neuropathy. Irreversible nerve damage. A side effect of her heretofore undiagnosed diabetes.

The burning hands and, later, feet, got so bad that she had to leave work and began sitting up all night watching television and eating peanut butter and jelly sandwiches. Their social life shrank to a dollar-menu dinner at a hamburger place every Saturday before going to sing karaoke at the Bavarian alehouse down the street from where they lived so Julius could exercise his vocal chords like in the old days, when he was still stupid enough to have dreams.

They held out as long as they could.

In the end, Julius was allowed to opt for early retirement with a reduced—much reduced—pension. They escaped Brooklyn just as November was turning bitter.

It was nice at first. Three hundred days a year of bright sunshine. Wide avenues lined with palm trees and neat, stucco-faced buildings. Every direction you turned there they were, red gold mountain ranges reflecting warm light down at an enchanted valley. Julius and Maura bought a dining room set and adopted a dog. They hit the buffets three or four times a week. Retirement suited Julius. He was a man who liked to go his own way.

But there were costs. The power bill alone could eat up two hundred bucks a month come summer. Then there was cable television. With all those night hours to fill, Maura ordered pay-per-view horror movies the way some people chain smoked cigarettes. It wasn't long before Julius began sending the phone company half payments and just covering the minimums on the two credit cards. Then came the night the cable cut off in the middle of *Die, Cadaver, Die* and all hell broke loose.

"What were you thinking?" Maura combed the check register, her forefinger gliding over entries, pausing to prod at gaps in check numbers and scribbled entries. "How can you write checks when you don't keep an eye on what's in the account?"

Julius tapped his temple. "It's all up here. Anyway, whoever heard of a hundred and fifty dollar cable bill? Why don't you read a book, for Christ's sake? I'll drive you to the library and you can take out as many as you want."

But turning pages made her fingers hurt, or so she said. Anyway, she got straight to the point. "You need a job, Julius. Why not apply at one of the casinos? Nothing drastic. Just for a few hours a week."

"Why don't you," he said and then could not look at her. She had liked working at One Police Plaza. She'd had friends. They'd eat lunch together in China Town and bring in cakes for each other's birthdays. Now, though, Maura could not work if she wanted to. And yet this did not change Julius' position that his days of wage slavery had ended.

Still, Julius did have the urge to get out of the house every so often. While he was hauling the recyclables to the curb one evening, he spotted a sign stapled to the light pole outside the house. The Patchwork Pony Bar and Grill was offering a hundred dollar prize for the best performer at their weekly Karaoke Night. Here was something to get excited about.

For his Las Vegas debut, Julius chose *Delilah*, and by the last chorus everyone in the house was singing along with him and Tom Jones. When he got back to the table, Maura told him he had the hundred for sure. It wasn't quite to be, however. In the end he split the prize with a Neil Diamond wannabe whose *Sweet Caroline*, Julius thought, was nothing out of the ordinary. Still, fifty bucks was fifty bucks. Julius was hooked. Over the next three months he and Maura never missed Karaoke Night. He even made a name for himself among the regulars.

"Aren't you the guy who sang *Unchained Melody* last week?" a bulky, barrel-chested guy in his sixties asked one night.

One of the women with him held out a bony hand, wrists piled with gold bracelets. "We really loved it. What a voice you've got." She turned to the other woman, a slightly younger blonde in a baby blue cowboy hat. "Darleen, this is the guy I told you about. Could've been on the original record."

Darleen widened her heavily made-up eyes. "Are you

singing the same song tonight? It's one of my all time favorites. Perfect for dancing slow and close together."

Julius pushed his shoulders back, trying to play it cool, but he couldn't help smirking. "I thought I'd try some Bobby Vinton tonight."

"Ooh—I know—" Darleen pursed her slick lips. "*She wore blue velvet whoa—whoa—*"

"*Bluer than velvet was the niiight—*" Julius didn't hear the DJ, Jay Fantasy, repeating his name until Darleen started shoving him toward the stage.

It was a good performance and, afterward, standing on the stage under the bright lights, staring down at the crowd of laughing people, Julius didn't mind that he had to split the prize this time with an Asian guy who'd murdered the Bee Gees' *More Than a Woman.*

Looking ahead for once in his life, Julius ignored Maura's lobbying for dinner and a movie and instead took his fifty bucks to a pawn shop downtown where he bought a used karaoke machine with a microphone and two sets of song discs.

"You planning to hire yourself out like Jay Fantasy?" Maura asked. She followed him through the living room. "'Cause if you are, Dorrie nextdoor has a grandson whose Bar Mitzvah is in a few weeks. They were going to hire a band, but I could give her a call."

"I'm not playing MC for a bunch of nerdy Jewish kids. '*Today I am a man,*'" he mimicked in a squeaky boy's voice. Panting, he set the equipment down in the kitchen to catch his breath. "I'm a serious singer."

"Yeah, right," she said, watching him swagger out to the garage to plan his set up.

By the next afternoon, Julius had his own sound stage. It wasn't long before he was hurrying through breakfast and heading for the garage. In his concrete-and-plasterboard cocoon, Julius felt at peace, channeling Bobby Darren and

The Tempations while Pancho-the-Chihuahua looked on benignly from the comfort of an old couch.

Halfway through Sinatra's *Fly Me to the Moon* he heard the bang-drag-bang of Maura making her way from the living room couch, across the kitchen floor, and toward his studio. Her bleary-eyed face appeared around the kitchen door, interrupting his finale.

"When are you going for lunch? I was thinking tacos."

It was eleven in the morning. His own breakfast still rested like a dead weight in his mid-section. But it didn't do to argue when he already knew the script. "Soon."

"By the way," she said. "I was on the phone with Dorrie this morning."

Julius turned on her, his microphone screeching. "I don't want to hear anything about her grandson's Bar Mitzvah."

Maura leaned heavily on her cane and shut her eyes, as if asking God for just a little more co-operation from the idiot she'd tied herself to. "This is about her son. He runs a security company. Mostly convention work at the big casinos. Twelve bucks an hour for checking name tags and directing people to the toilets."

He didn't say anything. Twelve an hour was not bad. And for all his reluctance to return to work, he knew they had to get a grip on their finances. Just two days before, he'd risked a speeding ticket to get down to the electric company in time to make a partial payment before they shut off the power.

"Dorrie's bringing over an application this afternoon. You just fill it out, and they'll send you for a drug test."

Julius shrugged his agreement and switched his Sinatra disc for James Taylor.

"Jesus—" Maura wrinkled her nose at the first strains of *Handy Man.*

He didn't think much of seventies pop-folk ballads either, but it was time to expand his repertoire. Jay Fantasy was hosting a special event to mark his 500th show at the Patchwork Pony. First prize was five hundred bucks. They'd announced the competition in the newspaper, so Julius knew he would be facing more than just Pony regulars. Singers would be coming from all over the valley. He supposed he could still spare an hour to interview with Dorrie's son and pee in a cup. It was nice to be the someone who knew someone for a change, the guy with the in.

If he thought caving in on the job front would buy him an evening's peace and quiet, Julius was to be sadly disappointed. At seven o'clock he came out of the bathroom shaved and showered, his best slacks laid out on the bed, to find Maura still in the grubby t-shirt and cut-offs she wore around the house all day. She hadn't even brushed her hair.

"You better get moving. We have to be out of here in fifteen minutes."

"I'm not going."

Julius pulled up his pants, closing the zipper with a determined yank. "Suit yourself."

Maura leaned on her cane with both hands. "I didn't sleep well last night. My head feels like it's splitting open and I think I'm getting the runs."

"You'll be okay." He ran a comb through his damp hair—God it was getting thin on top. "Are you getting ready or not?"

"I told you. I'm sick."

"Fine." He grabbed his wallet and keys. "I'll be back around one."

She blocked the doorway. "What am I supposed to have for dinner?"

"Whatever you want." He looked at the window behind the bureau. He could probably squeeze out into the backyard. Then he remembered that the gate was locked. "There's tuna. Have tuna."

"I'm sick of tuna." She turned sideways and he slid past

her. "I don't believe this. Here I am sick and sore and it's either go out with you or starve. Fine. But you'll have to wait until I get dressed."

Too late, he thought. As soon as he heard the rattle of a dresser drawer, he hurried down the hallway and out the front door. Pulling out of the driveway, Julius smiled at himself in the rearview mirror. He imagined the look on her face when she clumped into the living room fully dressed and found him gone.

It turned out to be the deadest night the Patchwork Pony had ever known.

Apparently NASCAR was in town. Not being a fan of car racing himself, Julius had no idea it was such a big deal, but there were no more than a dozen people at the Pony and none of them got up to sing. Jay Fantasy didn't seem bothered.

"I get paid either way," he said, scribbling down Julius' seventh song request. "And you've got your own show."

Sure. The Julius Bach Show. He might as well have been singing at a bus stop for all the pleasure it gave him. The house lights were on and suddenly he could see the gouges in the seat cushions and the crusty film on the poorly cleaned tables. His garage had more pizzaz. It would have been bearable if Darleen and her friends had at least shown up. They really could have made something of having the place to themselves.

When he got home, Maura was sitting in the den in the dark watching a repeat of *Psycho Cheerleader III*. She pretended not to notice him come in. The silent treatment.

He went into the bedroom to see what revenge she might have wrought there. His clothes were in the closet as always. His parents' wedding picture—a copy, the original had been torn to shreds and thrown in the trash after a previous battle—was on the bureau in its polished silver frame. He went into the bathroom and, picking up his brush and comb, gave them a tentative sniff. They seemed all right. Julius sank onto the bed and stared at his parents smiling back at him in black and white. Had he won?

It seemed he had. Maura never again attempted to get in the way of him going to the Pony. And to show his appreciation, he made sure to pick her up something nice for supper on the nights he went to sing.

Yet, on the night of Jay Fantasy's 500th show, Julius was tempted to ask Maura to order something in. He'd spent so much time choosing what to wear that he was running ten minutes behind schedule.

"Do you know what you want?" he asked from the bathroom, as he washed hands and face.

Maura, red-eyed and slow-moving thanks to another day spent sleeping until 3pm, nudged Pancho out of the way with her cane and scribbled something out on the memo pad next to the phone. *God*, Julius thought, *a friggin' list.* One pound Degrassi's Premium Genoa Salami, one half pound rice pudding, a loaf of bread, brown mustard.

He checked his wallet. Eleven bucks and three days until his pension check. Soon he'd be working for the security company, if they ever got around to doing the background check, but still.

"I don't think the deli counter is open this late," he said. "Why don't you order a pizza?"

"The sauce will bother my stomach. I called Shop-N-Save. The deli's open until eight."

It was seven fifteen. The contestants had to sign in at the Pony by eight. She wanted to fluster him. Make him rush so he'd screw up. No. He wouldn't screw up. He was good and she knew it. She just wanted to make him miserable. Julius slipped into his jacket and stuffed Maura's list in his pocket. He was going to win tonight. He knew it the way he knew the ground would be there when he stepped out of bed every morning.

He would stand on that stage and give them a show like they'd never seen before. And when he won, he would ask Darleen to help him blow his winnings. Steak and Champagne. Black Jack at the Bellagio. Now that was what he called a celebration.

There was a decided spring in Julius' step as he walked out to the car. He'd buy Maura her lousy salami. It was the least he could do. Because after tonight, everything would be different.

Interview With Lodi
Lynn Lanier

Wanda nervously glanced up and down the street as she stood in front of the massive glass doors of the 'Beliefs Are Us' building. The collar of her coat was pulled up to her ears and she wore a fashionable knit hat to disguise her red hair. However, it flowed from underneath and down her back, a dead giveaway if any of her friends happened to enter the block and look in her direction. She especially didn't want Father Flannigan to see her. He had warned her about this place.

    She saw strangers scurrying to their destinations to avoid the chilly wind funneling between the tall buildings, but she recognized no one. Satisfied, she slipped inside the foyer and confronted a video monitor telling her to look into the retinal scanner. Seconds later the inner door opened, and an android receptionist signaled for her to step to its desk. The inside of the building looked nothing like the exterior glass façade suggested. Its low ceilings, soft lights, dark blue carpet, and overstuffed chairs were more like a well decorated home than a workplace.

    She walked over to the desk and sat in the chair opposite the android.

    "What can I do for you, Wanda?"

Writer's Bloc III

"I'm sick and tired of people questioning my beliefs."

The android looked at the monitor sitting on the desk. "I see you're already maxed out on your 'Beliefs Are Us' virtual reality program. The law only allows you eight hours per week."

"Screw the law. People are laughing at me. I'm only happy when I'm living in the world with normal people."

"It's not the real world, Miss. The 'Beliefs Are Us' virtual world we created for you is constructed to match your idea of a perfect world. Let's see…" The android looked at his monitor. "You have a modified 1950's Middle American model with limited non-European interaction. Modifications include mid-twenty first century music and depictions of twenty-first century people you admire."

"Yes."

"You know we can't let you live there longer since it could damage your psyche. Besides, it's against the law."

"But I know Brandy Barnsworth."

The android quickly moved his index finger in front of his pursed lips and whispered, "Shh, don't mention that name out loud."

"Okay, but she said I could…"

The android quickly selected several numbers on his virtual keypad. "Please, Wanda, step through that door."

"What door?"

The android turned and pointed to the solid wall behind him. An opening appeared. Wanda stared in amazement.

The android said, "You obviously have plenty of money and know the right people. Go ahead; you've been approved."

Wanda walked around the desk and tentatively placed her hand on the opening. The opening is real, she thought. She stepped in and realized that it was an elevacar, which is an elevator that travels horizontally as well as vertically. She looked around. There were no buttons to push.

The doors closed, but they left no cracks – no sign that an opening ever existed. A few seconds later Wanda felt the car move, but there were no displays to indicate where she was going. She shivered when she realized she was heading into the unknown inside a box with no discernable features other than a ceiling that glowed with white light.

Five minutes later, the door opened. Wanda felt relieved; the ride seemed much longer than it was. She eased through the opening and peeked up and down the hallway. It had white lit ceilings, white walls, and a spotless white carpet, but no openings. A small box-like retinal scanner sprang out of the wall opposite the elevator. Wanda stared into the lens. Seconds later an invisible doorway opened. She walked through the opening and into an ornate office. Sitting at the massive carved rosewood desk was an elderly man.

"Sit down, Wanda," the old man ordered. "So, you want to spend longer in your idealistic world. Let me see…" He looked at a monitor that emerged from the top of the desk. "You have our modified 1950's model. Very popular. I suppose Brandy Barnsworth explained that it's against the law to extend your stay beyond eight hours per week because of the mental problems that causes."

"She told me of the mental stress, but it can't be more than I tolerate now. I'm not one to break the law, but all my friends are intolerant. They hate me because of my beliefs."

"We might be able to help you, but we have to be sure. I'm going to ask you a series of questions while we scan your brain."

"I don't believe in brain scans."

"It's mandatory, my dear. We cannot proceed without a psychological workup. We're doing you a favor, young lady."

Wanda thought for a moment. "Hmmm, I guess it's alright."

A helmet like object emerged from ceiling and slipped over her head. It fit like a glove.

"Are you ready," the old man asked. Wanda nodded. The old man held out his hand. "I'd like to introduce myself," he said. "My name is Lodi."

"You obviously know my name," Wanda replied.

"We know a great deal about you, Wanda. How does that make you feel?"

"I don't know. I guess I hadn't thought about it."

"Are you over the age of twenty-two?"

"I thought you knew everything about me." Lodi pointed at the helmet, but said nothing. "Okay, okay, I'm twenty-four."

"My records show you've logged 1034 hours of virtual reality sessions. You're aware the minimum hours for us to consider your candidacy is 1000 hours."

"Yes, I'm aware."

"I see you're still single. Have you considered marriage?"

"Why yes. I haven't found the right man."

"You understand that if you join our program, the man you marry will be virtual? We cannot subject another human being to your fantasy. Our purpose is to provide each individual customer with his own fantasy."

"What if our two fantasies are close?"

"We've never found two people who match closely enough for us to merge them. We've always found it better to create a virtual mate. Do you want children?"

"Why yes. I'd love to have children. I'd like to bring them up in a good Christian world, not that cesspool we call a world outside this building. All the hatred, killings, sinful sex, and the like…" Wanda leaned forward, laying her arms across the front of the desk. She stared into Lodi's eyes. "Sir, the world you people have created for me is so much better."

"You realize that in your fantasy world the children must be virtual like your mate. We cannot create real children and have them brought up in your idealistic world. Children must develop their own persona based on their own experiences. Have you thought about this?"

"Why, no I haven't."

"In the virtual world we create for you, you'll be able to date men and select the best one. It will feel like real love. You'll experience normal pregnancies, although our program will keep the morning sickness to a minimum, and you'll gain the proper amount of weight. You'll experience just enough pain of childbirth to make it seem real, but not too much to be intolerable. Your children will be perfect, except they'll get into a preset amount of trouble and require your motherly love and discipline. They'll grow into normal adults. You'll forget your husband and children aren't real. But you must know that when you die – they die with you since they're virtual. You will not leave a legacy. Do you understand this?"

"I guess so."

"You cannot guess. We cannot let you into our program it you're not sure."

"What about my belief in life after death? That's why people hate me now. I believe my soul will go to heaven after I'm dead. My friends don't believe that."

"Your beliefs are up to you, Wanda. We can design your virtual program so there's no conflict and everyone will accept your ideas as they are. We do not recommend that option, however. People who have tried it become bored and wish for the life they had before our program."

"I never intended to avoid conflict altogether. I just think there's too much in the real world. Can't you simply reduce the seriousness of the conflicts?"

Lodi looked at his monitor. "I see we've set the difference of opinion parameter for your weekly virtual reality sessions to 30% normal. Does that seem about right?"

"Yes it does." Wanda tried to move the helmet still firmly attached to her head. "This itches. Can I take it off?"

"Not until we're done. That brings up another issue, Wanda. Do you have any problems getting used to the virtual reality suit you wear during your weekly sessions."

"Not really. After a few minutes, I forget that I'm wearing it – especially the latest model. It appears you've fixed the defecation problem. God, the first time I had to go to the bathroom... What a mess."

"Have you had any problems eating or exercising?"

"The food tastes funny, but I'm used to it."

Lodi said, "Ah, you chose eating option 47A: nutritious food that looks and tastes decadent."

"Yes, I love that option. Will I age, Mr. Lodi?"

"It's just Lodi, Wanda."

"Will I age, Lodi. I mean... my physical body."

"Of course, but we offer several options. One, we can let your body age according to the lifestyle you choose. Our most popular option; however, is the one where we keep healthy no matter what you do. The 47A or equivalent eating program is mandatory with this option—we don't perform miracles. Our physical medical system will monitor your health and adjust your diet and exercise to keep you physically fit. You'll stay a size 2 for the rest of your life if you'd like."

"That sounds wonderful. But what do you mean by physical medical system."

"When you look at yourself in the mirror in virtual mode, you'll be looking at a virtual rendition of yourself based on your virtual life experience. For example, when you're pregnant with your virtual child, your actual body will not be pregnant, but when you look in the mirror, you'll look pregnant. The virtual medical system will inject you with appropriate hormones so you'll feel pregnant, but otherwise it will keep you at a healthy physical size 2."

Wanda shivered, but it wasn't cold. Something didn't seem right. She looked around the room. It looked like a normal executive office. The chairs were green leather, the plush carpet was gray, and the walls were paneled with rosewood that matched Lodi's desk. Light filtered through the windows, but there was no view of the outside world. Wanda noticed that the pictures on the walls were of clouds, oceans, and sunsets. There were no family portraits, and nothing of a personal nature on the desk or walls. The only thing on the desktop besides the monitor was a crystal decanter of deep red wine and two glasses sitting on a crystal tray.

Lodi said, "Wanda, we must talk about your death."

Wanda opened her mouth but didn't speak. She stared wide eyed at Lodi. A few seconds later, she said slowly, "My God, my death…"

"Just your death, for now, my dear; we'll talk about God in a few minutes. With our basic package, your body will live a normal life, albeit in the confines of our virtual reality equipment. At the age of about one hundred, your body will die normally, and your mind will die with it. Our firm will dispose of the body leaving no trace."

"Then will my soul be delivered into the hands of God? That's what Father Flannigan taught me."

"Your business, and our company tries not to interfere with them. We've found that a person's beliefs often change over time, and we attempt to adjust your virtual reality world to accommodate these changes. But we have the chicken and egg dilemma."

Wanda looked puzzled. "I'm afraid you've lost me."

"Our virtual world is bound to affect your beliefs, no matter how hard we try to stay neutral. We will not be sure whether our virtual reality program adjusts to your new beliefs or will be responsible for your new beliefs."

Wanda squirmed in her chair and began to finger the curls in her hair. "I have no idea what you're talking about, Lodi. Can't we go on to something else? I'm starting to have second thoughts about this whole thing."

"There is the matter of arranging your first death."

"First death? There's more than one? Too much death is one of the reasons I'm trying to leave the world I live in now. Can't we go onto the next thing on your list?"

"I'm afraid not, Wanda. If you sign up for the permanent program, we'll transfer you to one of our virtual reality modules. There you'll stay for the rest of your life. As far as the real world goes, you'll be dead. We must come up with a viable story that explains your disappearance. People that care about you will want to know what happened."

"Nobody cares about me. They all think I'm crazy."

Lodi looked at his monitor; its blue glow threw eerie dark shadows across his face. Wanda thought he looked like a vampire. He said, "My records indicate that fourteen people care about you, and another fifty-seven would be interested in your disappearance."

"That many? I didn't realize... Who are they?"

"I'm not at liberty to say. Shall we proceed with our standard disappearance scenario?"

"That's fine. I don't want to think about it anymore. But there's something that bothers me."

"Yes, Wanda?"

"You said my virtual children will die when I die. That doesn't seem right to me."

"Perhaps you'd like to consider our life after death option."

"That's what I've been saying all along, Lodi. I believe in life after death."

"No, you don't understand. It's not the spiritual life after death. When your physical body is near the end, we'll download all your memories into our LAD supercomputer. We'll design your mindscape based on your personal vision of heaven. You'll be able to witness your children and subsequent generations live their lives. Remember, you will not have a physical body, but as long as your mind is alive on our supercomputer, your virtual children will live."

Wanda started to perspire. Lodi reached into his drawer, pulled out a silk hankie and gave it to her. She wiped her forehead. She said, "Thanks," then flopped back in her chair. "Do you think my soul will go to heaven when you transfer my thoughts to the computer?"

"Are you alright, my dear? You look pale."

"I'm alright. I just feel a little dizzy."

Lodi looked at Wanda like a grandfather admiring his granddaughter. "I said before, Wanda, we're not in the business of interfering with your beliefs. We only attempt to facilitate your beliefs. We have nothing to say about spiritual life after death. We only offer the 'Beliefs Are Us' virtual reality version of life after death."

"Are we finished? Can I take this damned helmet off?"

"There's only one more topic that we need to cover. Are you up to it, Wanda?"

"I guess. Let's get it over with."

"If you're considering the mind download to extend your life, we recommend the early death option."

Wanda's eyes opened wide. She bolted upright in her chair. "What do you mean?"

"We would transfer your mind to our supercomputer soon after we finished with the paperwork and you complete the transfer of funds to the 'Beliefs Are Us' account. We would then allow your body to die. Your mind would live entirely in the virtual world created on our computer. We'd arrange for the police to find your dead body. It's much easier to explain a dead body than a disappearance."

Wanda jumped up and glared at Lodi. "You must be crazy. I must be crazy for coming here." She turned and stomped to the place she thought the door to be. She turned. "Open this door and let me out!"

"I'm afraid it's too late dear. You know too much."

Wanda rammed her shoulder into the door.

"Don't do that. I'm going to have to tell my security

people." Lodi pressed a button on his desk and the door opened. Wanda lost her balance and fell into the white hallway. Lodi stepped over her and quickly walked down the hall. Wanda got up, moved across the hallway, and started to pound on the wall where she thought the door to the elevacar was located. She ran her hands over the surface looking for a way to open the door.

The door popped open. She glanced down the white hallway. She saw Lodi turn. She quickly stepped into the car, and started feeling for invisible buttons. She frantically ran her hands up and down the walls of the car. She peeked again and saw Lodi hurrying toward the elevacar with a security guard. They were ten feet away. Wanda gasped and started to back away. Finally, the door closed. Wanda slumped against the wall. She almost fell when the car started to move.

She paced back and forth almost bumping into opposite walls. It seemed like an eternity. The door finally opened. She was behind the receptionist. Her mind cleared. She stomped up behind the android.

"Android, open the front door. I want to leave."

It pressed a button. The inner door leading outside opened. Wanda thought thank God, they hadn't notified it yet. She raced through the doorway. She pushed the exterior door. It wasn't locked. Wanda breathed a sigh of relief. She hurried though the door, turned, and started running down the street. The cold wind bit into her flesh, but she didn't care. She was free. She didn't stop running for six blocks.

Back at the 'Beliefs Are Us,' building, Lodi walked back into his office. A few minutes later, he heard a knock on the door.

"Enter," Lodi said.

The door opened and a priest entered, walked to the desk, and shook Lodi's hand.

"Welcome, Father Flannigan. Please sit down. Have a glass of wine." Lodi poured two glasses of red wine from the crystal decanter.

"I believe I will, Lodi. Thanks." Father Flannigan picked up his glass and held it up to Lodi. "It looks like you saved another soul, Lodi."

As he clicked his glass of wine against Father Flannigan's, Lodi said, "No father, we saved another soul."

Unhappy Friday
Linda Lou

Sharee greeted me with her full-of-the-devil smile as she loaded the coffee urn with a package of high test. "Good morning, Lindalicious!" she sang.

The "licious" part of my name is apparently a reference to a hip-hop song, so the twentysomething kids here tell me. As one of the oldest drones in this IT company—having marked the big 5-0—I'm flattered to have been given a nickname with such a young and flirty connotation. Better than "Crotchety Old Bat."

"Good morning, Ree-Ree," I answered. "Happy Friday! You going to the pub later?"

Sharee ran her fingers through her fuchsia-streaked hair, and then shimmied her sturdy build, momentarily turning the corporate kitchen into a late-night dance club. "Yay-yah!" she boomed.

Kristin, Sharee's best friend, works in the cubicle across from mine and my first order of business that day was to confirm Kri's happy hour attendance. "Oooh, yeah," she nodded.

Good. With the important stuff out of the way, I sat down to review the user interface guide I'd been working on for the past few days. I click... click... clicked through

Writer's Bloc III

the application, making sure I captured the step-by-step processes and wondering, for the millionth time, if God would be so cruel to put someone on this earth with the explicit purpose of writing software documentation.

This job is better than the last one, I have to admit. No more schlepping 24.8 miles every morning to the northwest side of town—what a pain in the ass that was. The traffic conditions were rarely favorable; usually I'd sit trapped in an automotive clusterfuck, bitching about being late for work because some idiot had to smash his car into a jersey wall, the 20-point rise in my diastolic blood pressure more of a concern than the possibility that someone might have been seriously injured. No, this job is much better. It's a lot closer to home and the guy I report to has no discernable mental problems, though I'd still rather be lying poolside counting the minutes until Guiding Light.

Click... click... click...

As always, I was thankful that day for the occasional distraction of Sharee's voice resonating throughout the cube farm. Whether she's gabbing about her plans for the weekend, the latest diet she's trying, or stories about her identical twin who works on the first floor, it's inevitably more interesting than the task before me. I get a kick out of my young friend and admire how she talks openly about her partner, Kimberli, just as others speak of their spouses. And why shouldn't she?

Click... click... click...

Lucky for me, my 2:00 functional spec meeting wasn't nearly as boring as it could have been, thanks to something from lunch that got caught in a back molar. I appreciated the distraction, and when my tongue finally dislodged what I determined to be a piece of chicken, I enjoyed a minor sense of accomplishment followed immediately by, so now what?

Afterward I headed back to my cell block, ready to announce that a mere hour and a half separated us from

Guinness time. But as I neared my desk, I saw Sharee in Kristin's cube, her body heaving with silent sobs, too overcome with emotion to emit a sound. Kri held her in a tight embrace, a futile effort to console the inconsolable.

What the hell?

I approached them, maintaining a respectful distance so as not to interfere. As I expected, Kri gave me a nod that communicated, "I'll tell you later," and so I retreated.

I bet they fired her, I thought. Loud, colorful personalities who occasionally address customers as "you guys" generally don't go over well in the corporate world. Hmm... I knew Sharee had had a wild night out earlier in the week and called in sick the next day. Maybe that did her in.

Poor thing. It's only a stupid job, sweetie. You'll find another one, a better one. I'll help you write your resume. You'll be fine.

Goddamn it, why did they have to get rid of her? My psychic communication shifted to corner office. Sharee's young—can't you give her a break? She's only a few steps down her career path, and she tries hard. Christ, I could think of five other people I'd ax before her.

We all mess around, I reasoned. The kids are always on Facebook and I never miss a day without checking the online obituaries of my hometown newspaper because—God forbid—what if someone from high school died and I didn't know about it?

Oh, no. What if...? With that thought, I reversed my initial position and hoped Sharee did, in fact, get fired, though I knew at that moment it wasn't so.

I discretely tried to assess the situation in the cubicle ten feet away and through a fringe of vision, I could see Kristin leading our coworker toward the exit. A few minutes later she returned alone, her face drained. My eyes pounced on her for information. Tell me I'm wrong, they said.

"Sharee's dad died."

"Had he been sick?" I asked, as if the pain would somehow be diminished had she seen it coming.

Kri shook her head. "No. He was killed in a motorcycle accident. On his way home from work. She's going to try to get a flight to Portland tonight."

We stood enveloped in a fog of sympathy, with nothing more to say. Kristin returned to her cubicle and shuffled papers, as did I.

My heart ached for our precious Ree-Ree as I thought of what she'd face in the days ahead—the trip home, the funeral arrangements, the exhaustion from the flood of tears—and I remembered when I got word of my own father's death. I was working on the road; my sister tracked me down at my hotel to deliver the news. "You're kidding!" I cried, as if her sense of humor had suddenly taken a sadistic twist.

A day can take the most unexpected turn; sometimes you go to bed to a picture that has no semblance of what you woke up to.

One of the software developers from the other side of the building breezed by on his way to the weekend. "Going to the pub, ladies?" he asked. After checking each other's reaction, Kristen and I nodded in unison.

At four o'clock we logged off and headed across the street.

And life goes on.

The Yesterday Before
Michael Molony

Thomas Flynn opened his eyes with a startled gasp. Confused and disorientated, he searched his room for familiar objects and patted his arms and chest as if to test his senses. He then held out his right hand and studied both sides, slowly turning it from front to back.

Thomas Flynn was a good man who had devoted as much time to his charity work as he had to his profession as an attorney. He now lay ailing in the bedroom he once shared with his wife, now six months deceased. The room was adorned with photographs washed in faded sepia tones capturing images of their experiences and adventures, their celebrations, their family, instances in time frozen and preserved with simple posed perfection. Most of his recollections were fleeting with old age and required prompting by a journal page, a picture or conversation with a friend. But one most deplorable incident, which happened when he was just a lad, was a memory he could readily recall.

His doctor, a lifelong friend and confidant, had determined his condition was quickly worsening and had asked the many guests and family members to allow his patient some rest. Everyone shuffled single file through the narrow doorway as the doctor drew the blinds and then shut the bedroom door behind him.

All except one, somehow left unnoticed.

A stranger emerged from a shadowy corner of the bedroom, hat in hand, and pulled a chair from beside the nightstand and sat down by the old man. The mellow amber light from a fire slowly burning itself out in the fireplace illuminated the visage of a tired and haggard man about the same age as Thomas Flynn.

"I had the most peculiar dream," the old man said, still looking at his hand.

The stranger leaned forward slightly.

"It happened so many years ago, but the memory has haunted me as if it were yesterday. What manner of harsh tricks a guilty mind places on a person unable to erase or redo an action for which one perpetually regrets."

He paused to gather his thoughts, to organize them in exact chronological order.

"When I was in the sixth grade at St. Andrew's School," he started; more relaxed now, "a new student transferred in to our classroom halfway through the school year. A girl, a very different girl... mentally retarded. Her name was Pamela, she was tall and lanky and who could have been several years older than the rest of us. She would try her best to participate in the games and activities with the other children, yet she was never accepted. For reasons of fear or resentment, the other children either ignored her or teased her mercilessly.

"After some time she gave up trying. During recess she would stand in the outer reaches of the playground talking to herself, having a full conversation in nonsensical rhetoric. I watched her, as I often did, drawn by her unusual style, yet frustrated as to why I couldn't help or understand her.

"'Is that your girlfriend, Flynnie?' a voice from behind me taunted. I turned to see a familiar gang of miscreants swaggering toward me. They laughed and snorted, slapping each other's hands in a ludicrous ceremony of congratulation.

"Without warning, one punk, Ty Barker, pushed me to the ground and then picked up a rock and hurled it at her. Like mindless minions, the others quickly followed suit, with two stones hitting her squarely in the arm and leg.

"'She's too stupid to even run away. What a retard,' Barker said, with a hateful laugh .

"'What's wrong, Flynnie? Don't want to hurt your girlfriend?' he taunted. She begged me with her eyes to help. Even having been stoned, she didn't cry.

"'Either you throw a rock, too, or you'll get a beating by all of us,' he threatened. The others started to surround me. I stood up and grabbed a rock, bigger than the others had used, and without a thought flung it hard. Fueled by fear, hatred and ignorance, and with disciplined accuracy, it struck her in the back of the head.

"A trickle of blood ran down her neck as she fell to her knees and wailed in pain, holding the wound with her hand. The boys hooted and hollered and I felt their contemptuous camaraderie as they slapped me on the back. In an instant I had defiled every tenant of chivalry and human nature, an action the memory of which I would never escape.

"The principal came out and the boys scattered. I stood frozen, as she looked at me, betrayed. The principal grabbed me by the shoulders and shook me hard. 'Just wait until your parents hear about this, Mr. Flynn,' he scolded. And that goes for your friends, too!' He dragged me up the stairs to the schoolhouse past a crowd casting their loathsome scowls.

"By some circumstance the other boys got away with impunity, claiming only one stone was thrown and that was mine. Pamela wasn't able or simply didn't want to speak of it; who would blame her? Anyone else who may have witnessed what happened was threatened into submission. It wasn't long before Pamela's parents pulled from the classroom and, as I was told, sent her to a home."

The stranger shifted slightly without saying a word.

"But wait, I have to tell you," Thomas Flynn continued, "In my dream just now, I know this must sound absurd, but I was back at the playground as a child once again. There she was, standing there in front of me just as she did that day, rubbing her hands close to her chest, conversing to herself. It was so real, so very real." The old man coughed weakly and then continued. "My memories and intellect were as I am now, but I looked at my hands and saw them small, fresh and smooth--devoid of lines and weathered skin. What's going on? I wondered.

"Instinctively I turned and saw the same group approach, led by Ty Barker. 'Is that your girlfriend, Flynnie?' he said on cue. They all laughed just as I had remembered.

Barker pushed me to the ground and again they picked up their stones and threw them at her. My one chance to stop them, and I lay helpless.

"'Either you throw a rock, too, or you'll get a beating by all of us,' he threatened as before.

There on the ground was the same large stone that I had thrown before. With maniacal intentions, I picked it up and squeezed it hard, staring straight at Barker with the antipathy garnered over many decades.

"'What you gonna do, chicken? Hold it or throw it?' he dared." Thomas Flynn closed his eyes with determination. "Even now, I can see his image--his round face sullied with dirt and sweat, his eyes squinty, his mouth full of crooked yellowed teeth.

"Voices in my head chanted in the name of righteousness and retribution. How good it would be to pummel this punk! I thought of all the oppressed children he and his gang had tormented and how I could now champion their emancipation.

"Barker must have sensed something because he swallowed hard and took one small step back. I stood up, looked him in the eye, and held my arm straight out in front of me. Then I opened my hand and let the rock fall to the ground.

"I turned my back to the gang, walked over to Pamela and wrapped my arm around her thin shoulders. Her dress of yellow paisley was neatly pressed and fitted, and I realized that someone cared dearly for this child and took the time to make her look pretty. Her auburn hair with crimson glints shifted in the sunlight and two tiny blue ribbons tied to form perfect pigtails, a style that all the girls wore. How much she wanted to be like the others.

"Rubbing her arm, she smiled 'Thank you' with her eyes in a language that transcended all intellects and cultures. 'Let's go inside, Pamela, and have the nurse check you out,' I said as I guided her to the front door of the schoolhouse.

"'That's right, Flynn, go help your girlfriend. You're a freak, just like she is,' Barker spat.

"Then, bam! I felt a sharp pain behind my ear, and momentarily lost my vision. A warm trickle of blood ran down my neck. Pamela wailed in horror as I had remembered, but this time out of selfless empathy. I knew without looking who threw that stone, but I chased the anger away and proceeded forward without turning around.

"'It's okay, let's just get inside,' I said passing the principal yelling, 'Hold it right there boys!'

"While the cowards scrambled, students and faculty had gathered. With faces confused and helpless, they parted a path as we climbed the steps. Standing at the top of the stairs was a man holding a towel.

"'I saw what you did, son,' he said. 'That was a noble thing to do.'

"I replied, 'Not noble really, that's just what people should do for one another.'

"He smiled and handed me the towel, motioning for me to place it on my head to stop the bleeding."

The stranger at the bedside smiled with keen sincerity. "That was quite a dream, Flynnie, a miracle maybe."

"Flynnie?" The old man thought for a second; he hadn't been addressed as such in years. "Forgive my lack of propriety, but I can't place your voice. My eyesight is poor these days." He raised himself up with as much strength as his curiosity could muster and looked closely at the stranger's face.

The stranger turned away slightly, but not before the old man recognized him.

Thomas Flynn's eyes opened wide, his face aghast. "My God, this can't possibly be…is this still some dream?"

"It's me, Ty Barker." He bowed his head, closed his eyes, and after a deep sigh looked up. With a contemplating breath, he said, "You see, Flynnie, you have been given an opportunity to relive an experience and prove to yourself that some of the errors of the past may be resolved. As children, we cannot benefit from the hindsight and experience earned with years. You were given a second chance to do the right thing, to not make the same mistake again."

"But Ty, that was easy. How I have often fantasized about changing my actions that day--to the point of overcompensating and apologizing through each charitable act I performed. I see now the selfishness of concealing my own guilt through charitable acts devoid of real sacrifice." Puzzled, he asked, "Did you think I would throw that stone again?"

"Not at Pamela. The real trial was whether you were going to throw it at me. You must understand the action would have been one in the same. But you let the stone fall to the ground – that was the real evidence of your convictions. Even after being struck, you still chose to ignore a rash instinct to retaliate."

Taken aback by this revelation, the old man had no

response. He knew how much he wanted to punish Ty, how close he was to repeating the same mistake. After some introspection, he realized that Pamela and Ty were in many ways very similar.

"What is it you want, Ty? Why did you come?" he said with a bewildered look.

"I came to apologize. What I did was wrong," Barker said earnestly.

Thomas Flynn raised and extended his hand. Ty, his face brightening, accepted the offer with both of his hands. The old man, recognizing the intentions as genuine, laid back slowly, closed his eyes, and at once felt completely at peace.

The door flew open and his oldest daughter, Margaret, busted in with the doctor behind her.

"I'm telling you, Bill, I heard him talking," she said, looking around the room for someone—anyone.

The doctor pulled the chair from beside the nightstand and sat at his friend's bedside. Taking Thomas Flynn's wrist, he felt for a pulse and then set it down carefully. He stared at the old man and reminisced about the good times they shared.

That's odd, he thought. In all my years of treating Tom, I never noticed a scar above his right ear. He touched it tentatively to convince himself of its existence, then slowly pulled himself up and placed his hand gently on Margaret's shoulder. She winced as the tears flowed down her face.

"No, no." she murmured, shaking her head slowly from side to side.

"He's gone, Margaret. You couldn't have heard anything. It was just your imagination. Everyone's been under tremendous stress. I'm sorry."

Surprised, Thomas Flynn found himself standing alone on the top step leading to the schoolhouse. The sky was overcast and a chilled breeze hustled the dry leaves along the pavement with the sounds of scampering mice. The old man squinted to focus. Intuitively, he held up his right hand and with casual acceptance recognized the weathered, grizzled look of age.

Looking down, he noticed a trail of fresh drops of blood leading to the doorway.

The metal door swung open and a young boy stepped halfway out to look at him, a boy he recognized instantly.

"Oh, good, you're still here. I forgot to thank you, mister," said the lad, holding a towel to the back of his head.

Thomas Flynn realized the man who had handed him the towel in his dream was, in fact, himself. In a strange and unexplainable contradiction of fate, he'd been granted an opportunity to see an alternate beginning of his new future.

"You're welcome, son, but you don't have to thank me." He bent down slightly and added, "That's just what people should do for one another."

The boy studied the old man as if he recognized something oddly familiar. After a slight hesitation he nodded with a timid smile and disappeared back into the schoolhouse, the door latching closed behind him.

It began to rain. With infinite complacence, the old man tilted his head back and closed his eyes to feel the water splash his face.

The bleeding drops of red were soon washed away, forever.

Silent Night, Holy War
(A Teaser of his upcoming book)
Kevin B. Parsons

CHAPTER ONE
Warehouse, North Las Vegas

Fahid stood still as a stone. This was the crux of the man's speech, he knew. Every man froze, listening intently.

"The time to crush the Great Satan is now!" Fahid stared at the speaker-phone expecting spittle to come shooting out of it. "We have made great progress through the past decade, from the USS Cole to the Embassy, the first World Trade Center attack, and our finest hour—9-11." Fahid smiled. The dozen men smiled and shifted nervously.

"I can assure you that this is no Twin Towers. No, but it is very much a second place, indeed. Just like the Twin Towers, we will attack in seven different cities at once. You did not know this until now. We needed to keep you from knowing it in case you were detained and interrogated. But tonight, there is no turning back."

Fahid looked at his peers. They stared back, surprised. None of them knew there would be other attacks. Yet, why not? Seven cities! Well, that generated seven times the destruction.

Fahid did not know the man. He knew only Nizar, his

contact. It did not trouble him. He understood the less information a person possessed, the safer it remained for the rest of the team.

"That was our greatest hour," the man continued, "the pinnacle of clever warfare! Using their planes as bombs to destroy their buildings and their people. This is similar, as we are using their legal product to destroy their buildings and people. The 9-11 attack killed almost three thousand people, while only nineteen of our own were martyred. We estimate this attack will kill approximately twenty-eight hundred, but will sacrifice only a hundred of our comrades. Heroes! You and I will make this strike and see each other in paradise tonight. A leader in each city has informed you of your duties. Do your duty faithfully and Allah will be pleased."

Fahid took a drag off his cigarette. The air in the small warehouse hung blue as every man nervously smoked. He still remembered that great day. What brilliance! For such a small investment of time, money, and people they annihilated multiple buildings, destroyed commercial airliners, killed thousands of infidels, and cast the Great Satan into a recession and fear like never before.

Yes, the Twin Towers. What an accomplishment. Fahid remembered when the first tower fell, self-destructing as the structural steel popped like firecrackers from the top to the bottom, annihilating itself downward and outward like a zipper. He remembered dancing in front of the television set, yet keeping his eyes riveted to the screen. Then, the great grey cloud of dust chased people down the streets of New York. He vividly remembered the fear and despair on their faces as they ran.

And, who could forget the many people jumping to their deaths from the buildings? It was truly much more than they ever expected. He smiled at his comrades. Praise to Allah!

"The beautiful thing with this attack is that we will hit their churches," the man explained. "And, we will do it tonight, on Christmas Eve.

"You know what to do," the man concluded, "Now, go and do it."

Fahid punched the button to end the call. He smiled at each man as he dropped his cigarette to the floor and crushed it out.

CHAPTER TWO
The Capstone Church, Las Vegas

> *"Silent night!*
> *Holy night!*
> *All is calm*
> *All is bright!"*

Hannah Brown started the singing. She stood center stage with a microphone, her voice a lilting balm to the ear. Pastor Jim Evans, standing beside her, chimed in to the traditional song. Their voices harmonized and inspired. They looked good and sounded good together.

Tanya Simmons in the twelfth row gently turned eight-year-old Bobby's head to face the front. Tanya knew the Capstone as a "church like no other," and how everyone focused on the show for Christmas. Not preachy, the Capstone created a welcoming place for people. That's why, in so many places, she could see the words "You Are Welcome" throughout the church.

Tonight, she could easily see that Pastor Jim loved to sing. The Christmas service, the faithful, the candles, the smells of the wax and fir boughs--it all made for a special evening. Tanya and her husband, Bob, picked up the words and sang as well. Soon, the song swelled and the church, packed with people this Christmas Eve, reached full chorus. The sweet, simple song filled every inch of airspace in the building.

Bobby Simmons wiggled next to his mom. This boy would require a little closer attention tonight, Tanya thought. Bobby was officially Robert Simmons III, but Bob and Tanya always called him Bobby. The three generations were Robert, Bob, and Bobby. She looked down at the blond head as he knelt on the floor and faced his pew holding his candle. Well, he wasn't disturbing anyone, yet. He wielded the candle like a sword. It did look like a sword, with the cardboard guard on it. The candle suffered at Bobby's hand. Bobby carved a groove down the side with his fingernail and chewed off part of the bottom. Tanya smiled. She remembered the taste of candles from her early memories of candlelight services.

She and Bob said he could have his own candle this year. Bobby suddenly looked up at his mother. He finally recognized the "candle song."

In the warehouse, the odd looking team prepared for the strike. Fahid dressed as Santa Claus while the rest donned fireman suits, their dark skin and eyes a contrast to the yellow hard hats. The team now worked in silence. They had planned this for two years, and everyone knew his job. Abdul walked up to Fahid.

"They will die tonight," he stated flatly.

"They will all die tonight," Fahid corrected, knowing what Abdul meant.

"Yes. But as long as your niece and my son die, I will be content."

"Abdul, that is not the mission," Fahid said, "Everyone dying is the mission. The only mission."

"I understand," Abdul nodded. "But, those two rejected their Muslin faith. They must die."

"They will. Only, everyone must die. Don't sacrifice the mission with your passion to kill only those two."

Abdul stared into Fahid's eyes. "I will not. I understand."

"Very well. That is why we chose this church."
Abdul nodded.
Fahid liked it being a wooden structure as well.
"Fireman nine to Santa Claus," the radio squawked.
Fahid rolled his eyes at the idiotic call names.
"Yes, go ahead," he spoke into the radio.
"Everyone is in place. Ten inside, six outside."
"Very well," Fahid replied, "We are leaving soon."

Fahid finished putting on the Santa suit. He called it the Satan suit, but didn't speak of it, now. Jakar and the other four looked at their handiwork. The pick-up looked foolish decorated with Christmas lights, garlands, and tinsel. Fahid hated to die dressed like this, but he hoped Allah would understand. Everyone stood in a circle in their fire suits, complete with gloves and boots. They removed their helmets and carried them. Each man looked overinflated in his fireman suit. Now, they were ready. Time to go. But first, his speech.

"Silent night!
Holy night!
Shepherd quake
At the sight."

Tanya heard the song swell throughout the church. She saw Pastor Evans and Hannah Brown standing on the little stage with their candles. They both passed the flame to two ushers each. The little fires spread slowly, but soon gained speed as two passed to two more, and so on, until the entire church glowed in amber hues.

Tanya remembered how they built this church. She and Bob had been with Jim Evans since the beginning, before they were married, or dating, for that matter. The church grew like the candlelight. One to two, two to four, and so on. The light barely grew, then lit the place exponentially as sixty-four lit one hundred twenty-eight.

She remembered Jim's vision. His eyes danced as he told them of his vision of a church in Las Vegas, bigger and better than any other church.

"The only reason it will be bigger," he would say, "is because it's better. We want to reach people and introduce them to Christ and have Him dramatically change their lives." He imparted that vision to his flock of fifteen. Every man and woman believed it to the depths of their soul. She watched Jim singing with Hannah and smiled.

Jim was like that, Tanya mused. He could spark a vision and sense of destiny in anyone, and they would believe and act on that belief. As a whole they became greater than their parts.

Jim talked about 'critical mass,' a point where the church grew and then took off like it was shot out of a cannon. Tonight, Tanya could feel it. *We are almost there. I know it.*

No one impacted her like Jim Evans. His passion and drive were unmatched. Tanya was delighted to be on Pastor Jim Evans' team.

The fifteen original people told their friends, who told others, and so on. They made "You Are Welcome" their motto right from the start. Tonight, it showed. Now, they provided three services, two tonight and one early tomorrow. This was the first, this one filled to overflowing. The midnight one and early Christmas morning would be full as well. If the fire department came, they would send people away, but they looked the other way on an event such as this.

Tanya gently reached for Bobby's hand. It was time! She touched her candle to Bob's and then turned to Bobby. He held his up to hers. Magically, his candle lit. He held it in front of him. Then, Tanya pushed his arm to encourage him to light his neighbor's. Bobby watched the glow and looked up at his mother. His face glowed, an amber hue, like a little angel's. Tanya watched Bobby wiggle his candle left and right. The wax drooled down to the cardboard.

"Be careful with the fire, honey," she chided gently. She remembered the one time he stole matches from the house and played with them in the backyard. He burned his thumb badly and ran into the house, crying and confessing his indiscretion. He really got in trouble that time. So, she knew he must be careful. Even the wax was hot! But, she remembered the simple joy of watching the flame dance on the wick and melt the wax.

"...holy war!" Fahid finished the speech. The words certainly didn't match the Santa suit. The others stood in their firefighting gear. They all knew why they were here and what the mission required, but Fahid's speech would solidify their resolve. He looked in each man's eyes, and they appeared ready. Each man stared back intently, their eyes determined yet edged with fear. Each possessed plenty of weapons and ammo, plus the steel bars and chains. One man inside each exit, one outside, two inside and outside the main entrance, one remote man, and Fahid driving the little truck. The simple plan would cause extensive damage to the Great Satan. As he dismissed the men, each team got into various cars. Fahid and Jakar entered the little Chevy S-10.

Calmly, Fahid drove the old white pick-up out of the warehouse. The engine rattled, and it smoked a bit. Surely, it could go the distance, however. The cars split off in different directions, but with a common destination. Fahid and Jakar would stop at the gas station across the street and fuel up. That would take awhile.

"Holy night!
All is calm,
All is Bright!

Yes, and the glowing candles indicated this as well. Tanya

looked around, smiling at her friends. She saw Pastor Evans smile at Hannah, singing beside him onstage. Wow, could she sing. Hannah and Pastor Jim harmonized together so well. Perhaps, some of the "touchdown people" (that was what they called the ones who touched down at Christmas and Easter) would really hear the song and understand. Tonight the church reached out to many who were unavailable the rest of the year. Pastor Evans always gave a short sermon at Christmas, and not too preachy. She appreciated that. They didn't want to drive people away.

They always repeated the first verse at the end to underscore, to let it sink in. Tanya reminded herself of the Lord's family. Forced to go to Bethlehem for a government mandated census, Joseph and Mary trudged to Bethlehem while she was fully pregnant. Mary gave birth to the Christ child in a little stable that night.

Tanya watched Bobby's candle get smaller, yet the flame flickered brightly. He must have thought Mom wasn't watching as he swept his finger over the flame. Last year, he asked about the song, because he didn't understand it. Who was 'Round John Virgin'? He told her it sounded like one of Robin Hood's merry men. Tanya laughed and tousled his hair and told him that was a different story.

As Jakar filled the tank, Fahid entered the store. The white fluorescent lights assaulted his eyes. A bell chimed as the door opened. Why did these infidels have to overdo every single thing? A Christmas carol played tinnily.

Fahid shook his head before realizing it was out of character. Better watch that! The shelves spread before him jammed with food. The magazine racks displayed a constant evil barrage of flesh. These infidels were so superficial, lazy, and prosperous. With the endless onslaught of crap on the shelves, it would be easy to shop slowly, and then, talk to the clerk as the fueling continued. Good, it was a woman. The brainless one would be easy to distract.

Seventy virgins is the promise for a martyr, Fahid thought as he approached to talk to this whore. She certainly wouldn't be one of them. She wore a low cut, tight, black shirt that he couldn't divert his eyes from, with a butterfly tattoo on her left breast. A rock band name stretched across her chest in gold lettering. The short shirt and low pants revealed her white midriff. Both ears claimed at least six piercings, her right eyebrow laced with a little pin. Her coal black hair contrasted the pale white skin and dark red lipstick. Disgusting. He did the best job of acting like Santa he could, but it was pretty weak. He knew "Ho-Ho-Ho," but that was about all.

"Santa! You're early! Do you have a present for me?" The female batted her eyelashes at him.

"Oh, um, not yet. It is too early," he stammered.

"Well, don't forget me. I'll be waiting for you." The girl smiled seductively.

"Ah, well, I will be there," he assured her. What an infidel. He would love to pull his pistol out of the Santa suit and shoot her dead, but couldn't risk compromising the plan. Just keep her entertained while Jakar is fueling. Fahid paced nervously. What if the radio gave them the signal? He remembered the three minute window, at least, from their survey of the service last year. What if the order changed, or they didn't do it like last year? Calm down, it will go according to plan.

"...Mother and child.
Holy infant so
Tender and mild."

Tonight, Tanya saw families all around. Husbands and wives embracing, parents holding their children's hands, the amber glow of their faces in the candlelight looking so angelic. Usually the kids attended Sunday school, but tonight was family night. She remembered candlelight services from being a little girl, like the first time she could hold the candle herself. Her mother monitored her closely as she could hardly cease wiggling through one song. She remembered wondering if her coat would catch fire if she held it under her sleeve.

This slut is just a child. In this hateful country their evil behavior even extends to the very young. She told Fahid a dirty Santa Claus joke. The guilt he felt for the young children destined to die tonight evaporated. Along the wall stood a row of slot machines. He saw them everywhere. This Las Vegas--the term Sin City was right! A guy sat, smoking and feeding a machine. He should shoot him, now. Stay focused on the mission. Come on Jakar; how long will this take? He must be patient. Better make some conversation. He couldn't think of anything else, so he posed the traditional Santa question.

"Have you been a good girl?"

The girl leaned over, her breasts on the counter. He could see a long way down her shirt, past the butterfly. Finally, he dragged his eyes away and looked in her eyes. She smiled.

"Oh, Santa, I've been real good." She winked.

Sweat broke out on his forehead. He smiled.

"Sleep in heavenly peace.
Sleep in heavenly peace."

Now, the entire church glowed with the amber tint of the candles. How peaceful! "Thank you, Lord, for coming into my life," Tanya prayed. The music soothed her soul.

"Fireman one to fireman nine," Jakar spoke into the mike.

"Go ahead," crackled the reply

"We are ready to execute in two minutes."

"We are as well."

Jakar caught Fahid's eye and waved to him. He exited the store.

In the truck, Fahid and Jakar looked at each other. The radio continued to crackle affirmatives from the others. Fahid jammed the little truck into gear, and they crossed the street, laboring under its heavy load. Fahid stopped a hundred feet in front of the church entrance and let Jakar out to run behind and cover the doors. Fahid revved the engine and drove straight for the entry of the church. He left the cap off the tank and gas sloshed out the top, making it better. The engine screamed. The little white truck crashed through the door, splintering wood and twisting steel.

Fahid charged down the aisle toward the front of the church, carrying the huge fuel bomb. The congregation held the 556 igniters in their hands. Tanya heard the crash and turned to look. Suddenly, she saw a white truck flash by Bob. Santa Claus? Driving a truck into the church?

The initial explosion sent a ninety foot fireball through the center of the congregation with a loud boom. Almost immediately, the pick-up exploded from its fuel tank. The dragon flames consumed seats, carpeting, pews, and people. The closest victims vaporized instantly. Further out, people burned quickly. Outside that area, others watched in horror as the fire grew rapidly, consuming seats, clothing, and celebrants.

Tanya saw the flash and flame, much bigger than her little candle. As her final act of love, she covered Bobby to protect him from the flames, giving him just short of three seconds more time living than his mother and father.

Seductive
Debbie Prince

I loved the way her mouth formed a kiss when she said the word "painting." The woman slinking into the art gallery that fine day gave "nice" a new meaning. She called herself Irene and if she'd handed me a rope, I would have hung myself. I listened intently to her tale of whoa, how her mother's lover, now on his deathbed, decided to sell his worldly goods. I wasn't blind to the truth, I just chose to see the truth differently.

Irene described the painting, one of the lost Giacometti's, in absolute mint condition. I couldn't help but think how she looked like the masterpiece's work herself. Long slim shapely torso, sheathed in a dress so tight, she couldn't laugh without busting a seam.

Irene didn't have the painting with her. She'd had to take the bus and if I wanted to see the artwork, I'd have to drive her to her house. "Come up and see my etchings?" she asked with a seductive wink of the eye and then a little laugh to show me that she did have a sense of humor.

I would love to come to her bedroom and I would love to see her etchings.

I grabbed the keys to the jaguar, locked the gallery door and led her out the front. She followed me down the dark alley to the back of the building. I found the Jaguar. She got in without hesitation and directed me to her house. We passed the tony shops of Beverly Hills and continued a number of blocks until she told me to turn in to a tree-lined street lined with mini-mansions and a few crumbling behemoths. The street screamed of old money being run out by new money. We pulled up in front of a large Spanish Villa, overgrown with Ivy and untrimmed hedges.

She had to boost the heavy front a little with her shoulder. I imagined cobwebs and white-sheeted furniture. But I never imagined what I did see.

A corpselike figure sat in a easy chair, staring at me. The skeleton so startled me that I jumped back, with a sharp intake of breath.

"This is Andrew," she said simply, dropping her keys on the table by the door.

I did not expect anybody to be there.

The emanciated man nodded to me but did not say anything.

"There's a bathroom in there, if you'd like to freshen up." Irene's heels made clacking noises as she continued down the hall.

I skirted past the man, charging for the safety of the bathroom. My pale face starred back at me. I had to get a hold of myself. What could one cadaverous senior do to a man of my stature? I grabbed the toothpaste with shaking fingers and finger-brushed my teeth, wiping away the stink of Cajun Garlic chicken that I'd unwittingly wolfed down in the Gallery's office. I threw cold water on my face and washed my hands. In the short time that I'd seen the man, I'd already chewed at my cuticle, drawing blood without even realizing it.

I heard a squeaky sound and I imagined the old man out there sharpening knives. I opened the window to let some of the warm California air revive me and I saw the source of the squeaks. One of Irene's eccentric neighbors had tacked an old weather vane to the roof of his house. I took one last relaxing breath and stepped out of the bathroom.

The old man had vacated his chair. Irene stepped out of the bedroom at the far end of the hall. "I'm in here." Her sultry seductive voice lulled me like the siren's call. I forgot about the old man and walked toward her, trying to slow down the cadence of my walk. I was supposed to be the sophisticated Devin Flanagan, owner of the elite Flanagan Art Gallery, not some pig running to its slop.

She turned into the bedroom with a nice swing of her hips and a slight turn of her head to make sure that I followed.. Like a dog on a sirloin steak trail, I followed..

"Is the painting in here?" I asked, teasing her.

She must have been afraid that I would turn the light on, because she stopped me with two feather-light hands on my shoulders. Her eyes widened in surprise. I'm sure I was more muscular than she thought an art gallery owner would be.

We stood like that, until my eyes adjusted to the light and I could see the painting leaning against the bed.

She took my jacket off with a deft lift of her hands, distracting me.

"So you like?" she asked, gently nibbling on my lips.

"Oh yessss," I moaned, my knees going weak.

"I'm going to need the money," she pouted, holding back a little.

I expected this. I fumbled a little with my jacket and found the check that I'd torn out of the gallery's book. I made the check out for enough money to buy a small house in this town and carefully signed Devin Flanagan's name. I held the money above her head playfully. She enticed me with a little wiggle and I wedged the check down the front of her dress. After that I could not stop myself, and for the life of me, I do not know where that check went. She knew more maneuvers than all the women I'd been with combined. Sweat lined my back and my breath came out in short rapid bursts by the time she finished. It's a wonder that I remembered to pick up the painting.

She walked me to the door, her arm linked in mine. "I've got more. Would you like me to come by the Gallery tomorrow?"

I hadn't expected this and I had to think fast. "I think the gallery is quite sated."

She laughed at my choice of words, but did not walk me to the car. That suited me just fine. I placed the painting in the back of the Jaguar. It was beautiful, but it was a fake. I could see when the bright California sun exposed the cheap house paint the forger had used and the signature was too perfect for the impatient Giacometti to have scrawled. I smiled sadly for her and got in the Jaguar, pulling away carefully. I drove for about a mile, careful not to break any traffic rules.

I left the car, the painting, and the checkbook in a strip mall parking lot five miles from the Gallery. Sorry, Devin, but I will need the suit for a little while and you will not.

Barring any calamities, I would be in Mexico before nightfall and the only thing they would find in the Gallery was Devin's empty shell.

Those Oldies but Goodies
Donald Riggio

Old Doc Weidmann's death wouldn't be front-page headline news in The Daily News or even The New York Post for that matter. The seventy-year-old proprietor of Doc's Candy Store in the Fordham Road section of the Bronx didn't warrant such citywide media attention. But if you lived in that area at any time during the last five decades, Doc's place was legendary.

Groups of teenagers gathered there daily to enjoy such soda fountain favorites as malteds made with real powdered malt, egg creams made without eggs, and black and white ice cream sodas. My era to hang out at Doc's was the mid-sixties.

It was there, amid wrought iron tables and chairs that flanked a Wurlitzer jukebox, that I asked Carmela Pininni to go out with me when we were both fifteen, and it was there seven months later that she broke it off. Another vivid memory occurred three years later in sixty-five when Doc let me, Joey DeMarco, and Alan Frank sit in the place till way past midnight, because we were shipping out for Vietnam the next morning.

By nineteen sixty-eight, Joey and I were back, but Alan never did make it home. I entered the Police Academy a year later, and after graduation, I was assigned to the neighborhood precinct and walked a beat taking me past Doc's store several times a day. Mrs. Weidmann always offered me a cherry-lime ricky or a soft, salted pretzel almost every time I came around the corner. I guess, now, I can admit to taking her up on her offer on more than one of those hot, dog days of August.

I got transferred to the Northeast Bronx in seventy-six and made detective in nineteen-eighty, so my trips to the old neighborhood were relegated to the times I went back to visit my mother. Mrs. Weidmann was gone by then, but whenever I drove by, I'd still see a few familiar faces, like Lenny Hayes. Lenny was some five years my senior. The kids in my crowd knew Lenny was slow, didn't play with a full deck, we used to say. His belief that, as a holdover from a prior generation, he had some kind of power and authority at the candy store was more imagined than actual fact.

My buddies and I got into a beef with him one time, because we asked Doc to put some Beatles songs in the jukebox. Lenny was a DooWop fan and didn't want any of his old fifties tunes taken out of the Wurlitzer.

"Nobody better mess with my music," he'd warn.

"C'mon, Lenny," someone told him, "Give us a break, man, those tunes are ancient."

Leave it to Doc to employ the Wisdom of Solomon by removing records by the likes of Perry Como and Patti Page to make way for the Beatles. That made my crowd happy and kept Lenny quiet.

My mom passed away in eighty-nine, and I hadn't been back since. Now, it was nineteen ninety-seven and I was Chief of Detectives. I was on my way downtown to One Police Plaza when the call came over the squawk box at about 7:00 a.m. I immediately recognized the address. A dead body had been found. I feared it might be old Doc.

I detoured my Crown Victoria off the New England Thruway at Mosholu Parkway and then to the Southern

Boulevard exit. When I turned onto Arthur Avenue, there were already two sector cars on the scene as well as an unmarked detective's vehicle and an EMS ambulance.

After I rolled up and got out of the car, I took a long look around the area and was somewhat shaken to see how much the old neighborhood had deteriorated. This gave the uniformed officer stationed at the door enough time to poke his head inside.

"Brass!" He called to his brother officers inside.

His warning meant that when I got inside I'd find all police personnel going over the crime scene with total, by the book precision.

"Good morning, sir," the same officer said to me as he stepped aside to allow me to enter.

"Morning." I nodded a greeting as I entered the store.

It was like stepping through a time portal. Aside from the police activity, the place looked just as I'd remembered it, the finely tiled floor, the tables and chairs, and of course, the jukebox. I'd been correct in my assumption about what I'd find on my arrival. All the cops were busy at work, all except for one young, Hispanic uniformed officer. He sat on one of the upholstered stools, his elbows propped up on the counter, and the index fingers of both hands kneading his temples. His uniform cap sat upside down next to him.

I looked passed him to the two plainclothes detectives standing at the far end of the counter in the rear of the store. A body lay on the floor at their feet covered by a sheet. Both detectives looked to be in their forties, a salt and pepper team, one black, the other white.

As I approached, the black officer nodded my way. "Chief."

His partner attempted a clumsy, two fingered salute that embarrassed him and might have, under different circumstances, caused me to chuckle.

I knelt down next to the body and pulled away the top

of the sheet. It was Doc Weidmann all right. There were several bruises on his face and neck. I've seen more than my share of corpses, but it saddened me to see the body of this kind old man who meant so much to me in my youth. That he died as an act of violence angered me. I replaced the sheet over his face and stood.

"What's it look like?" I asked the detectives.

"The beating doesn't appear to be all that severe, but with a man his age," the black detective made his report, "it coulda' been the blows that killed him…the fall…maybe, his heart just gave out. The coroner won't commit to anything yet."

"Robbery?" I asked.

The white plainclothesman now spoke. "Doesn't shape up that way. We found a paper bag with about three hundred dollars in bills and coins next to the body, probably his start-up cash. The rookie that found the body says he didn't see anyone—there was no sign of forced entry. Looks like whoever did this just had an argument with the old guy— knocked him around and then took off."

These two were good cops; I could see that. But, I could also see that neither of them put a very high priority in Doc's death, and that the whole matter would probably end up on the bottom of their case file soon after it was written up. I couldn't have that.

"Listen, no reflection on you guys, but I'm going to be poking around this one."

"Did you know the victim, Chief?" one of them asked.

"Yes. I did. He had family…two sons…out on Long Island, I think."

"The rookie gave us that information, sir. We made the necessary notifications. Someone will be in to identify the body."

"Good." I gestured to the young policeman seated at the counter. "Is that the rookie?"

"Yes, sir, Officer Ruiz."

I turned from them and moved to take a seat next to the young cop. "You okay?"

My words startled him, and when he looked at me, my rank flustered him.

"Oh, er yes, sir. I'm sorry, sir; it's just that…you see, I'm the one found the body and…I'm from this neighborhood. I've known Mr. Weidmann since I was a kid."

"I understand. The detectives tell me you didn't see anyone hanging around when you arrived on the scene. That about right?"

"Yes, sir. When I'm on this tour, I try to swing around and help old Doc open up. He sometimes had trouble with that heavy gate out front."

"Back when I was hanging out here you didn't need a big heavy gate. Locking the front door was enough," I explained.

"I guess a lot of things have changed since then." The rookie commented, and then continued his report. "My partner and I were ticketing a speeder over on Pelham Parkway, so I was delayed in getting here. When we arrived, I noticed the gate was only part way up and the morning papers were still tied up and stacked outside just where the deliverymen left 'em. I knew then something was wrong. I came inside and found Mr. Weidmann lying there. I checked the back door to the alley and the window in the lavatory. They was closed and bolted like always. Nobody coulda' come in or out that way."

"You did a fine job, Ruiz," I said. But, that didn't help console the young cop any.

"They don't think we're gonna' catch this guy do they?" He gestured toward the detectives.

"They know I have a personal interest in this; they'll make the effort."

"I better get back outside and help my partner with the locals."

Ruiz put his cap back on and headed to the front door. I walked along with him. There was indeed a small crowd of curious onlookers gathering outside. It was then I noticed a familiar figure pacing back and forth across the street.

"Is that Lenny Hayes over there?" I asked, not sure why I thought Ruiz would even know who he was. But, he did.

"Yeah, that's him."

Aside from the green, silk jogging suit and white, designer sneakers he wore, Lenny looked the same. He still wore his hair, now gone silver gray, in a slicked back style with a pompadour curling down the front of his forehead. To be honest, it looked rather silly, but at least, he still had a full head of hair, which was more than I could say for myself.

"Ever had any problems with him?" I asked Ruiz.

"Not really, nuisance stuff mostly. He's always getting into shouting matches with some of the local teenagers, yelling at them for playing their boom boxes too loud, criticizing the music they listen to. But he's been doing that for years."

"Does he still live over on One Hundred Eighty-seventh Street?"

"No, they tore down most of those apartment buildings a year or so ago. They moved his mother into a new senior citizens complex on Arthur Avenue. I'm pretty sure he flops there with her."

This Ruiz kid had the makings of a fine cop, and I was always happy when I came across a young man like that. I let him go back to work and then went back into the candy store.

I kept out of the way of a team from the Medical Examiner's office that were preparing to move Doc's body from the scene. It had indeed been a long time since I investigated a crime scene, but my instincts took over and I mulled over what we knew about Doc's death.

It was probably an accident, committed by someone

Doc knew. I strolled across the floor to stand in front of the jukebox. My eyes glanced down and scanned the song titles contained in the music machine and a sudden realization popped into my head. The realization formed into a theory, a long shot to be sure, but in a case devoid of any leads, it was a theory worth exploring.

I hurried outside and looked out over the ever increasing crowd. When I didn't see what I was looking for, I sought out Officer Ruiz. I found him a short way up the block near his radio car.

"You got any idea where we can find Lenny Hayes right now?" I asked him.

"Sometimes, he hangs out over at the old playground. Why, what's up?"

"I want to have a little chat with him. Take me for a ride."

"Yes, sir."

We got into the patrol car. Ruiz was smart enough to not ask any more questions, and we drove the four blocks to the playground on One Hundred Eighty-third Street in silence. I was troubled to find the playground had been closed down. A tall, eight foot chain link fence had been erected to keep people out. The wooden seesaws were gone, and the monkey bar set was broken, reduced to a mass of twisted metal—the asphalt surface dug up in huge chunks.

"There he is." Ruiz had been correct. Lenny sat with his back to the street on what was left of a wooden bench just inside the fence. He'd gained access through a break in the links large enough for someone to squeeze through.

"Pull up there, on the opposite side of the street, and park," I instructed the rookie, who complied without question. Once we were parked, I started to get out.

"Want me to go with you?" Ruiz asked.

"No, I can handle this."

I made my way across the street, clumsily maneuvered

my way through the break in the fence, and came up behind Lenny. I wasn't sure how he'd react, so I spoke quietly and cautiously.

"How's it going, Lenny?" He snapped his head around, but there was an instant look of recognition in his lined face. Getting this closer look at him made me realize that the years had not been as kind to him as I'd previously thought.

"Hey, what do you say there?" He greeted me like we still saw one another every day of the week.

"When did all this happen?" I motioned toward the rubble.

"Ah, about six months ago. The kids wasn't really using it anymore, the junkies and dealers took it over. So, the city just busted it all up."

"A shame."

"Yeah, I guess," Lenny muttered. I still wasn't quite sure he knew who I was until he asked. "My moms says you're some kinda big shot cop these days?"

"A Chief," I said.

"A Chief, huh? You got a cigarette, Chief?"

"I gave 'em up a while back."

"Ahhh, I should quit myself. My mother says the secondary smoke bothers her emphysema. Secondary smoke, can you beat that? I didn't have to worry about crap like that when we was living at four forty-five. I had my own room then. Did you know they tore down all those buildings over there?"

"Yeah, I heard."

"Man, that was a great place, big lobby, great echo. You know, Dion and his guys used to sing in our lobby before they made it big. Did you know that?"

"Yeah, sure." I humored him. Every kid who came from the area claimed Dion and the Belmonts sang in their hallway. I think I even once tried to impress my own kids with that story when they were young. But since neither of them had the slightest idea of who Dion was, they weren't impressed at all.

Lenny continued, "Now, I sleep on the couch in my mom's apartment in the senior citizens place, and she busts my chops about secondary smoke. Unbelievable, right?"

I thought it was a good time to change the subject.

"You know, Lenny, I'm looking into what happened over at Doc's this morning. You heard about that, didn't you?"

"Yeah, yeah, it's terrible. I suppose they'll close that place down now too, huh?"

"I guess so. I was checking things out in there before, and Lenny, I got to ask you something. When did they take all the old songs out of the jukebox?"

"About a week ago," Lenny answered somberly.

I needed to hear more.

"That must have made you pretty mad?"

Lenny nodded his head and lowered his gaze to the ground. "Doc had been talking about doing it for a long time now. He said he was losing money...that the kids was coming in and playing their radios instead of the jukebox, because they didn't like the songs that were in it. How could he be losing money? Jesus, if I could get back all the nickels and quarters and dollars I pumped into the friggin' thing over the years, my mother and me could buy a condo in Florida. But you know Doc, always for the kids, had to do what the kids wanted. But, what about me, I was a kid once, what about me?"

He spoke more out of guilt than anger. Tears welled up in his eyes; he fought them back as he continued to wrap up the mystery.

"First, they take away my room, tear down our building and move me and my mom into some piece of crap senior residence where I can't even smoke. Then, even old Doc turns on me and takes my songs away." He was now able to look me in the eyes. "I only went there to talk to him, I swear.

But, he just kept saying there was nothing he could do, and I went off. I hit him a couple of times, and he fell on the floor, hard. You know me, man, I'd never do anything to hurt old Doc. I loved the guy."

Lenny hung his head and sobbed.

"I believe you, Lenny. But, you understand I need you to come with me down to the station house, and when we get there, I want you to tell Officer Ruiz everything you just told me, okay?"

Lenny just nodded.

I knew my decision to give the collar to the rookie patrolman would annoy the two detectives working the case, but with Ruiz being from the neighborhood and a friend of Doc's, I figured he'd feel good about taking part in solving the case.

"I should go up to my mom's place and tell her what's going on so she won't be worried about me," Lenny said.

"Sure, I nodded in agreement, "But, you understand, I gotta' go with you."

"Oh, that's no problem," he answered as he stood. We turned and headed toward the patrol car. "After all, you're an old friend from the neighborhood. My mother will be glad to see you."

Somehow, I didn't think she would.

Jenny and the Model T Ford
Nancy Sansone

Sixteen-year-old Jenny Smith drove down Grand Avenue in the familys almost new, shiny black, 1927 Model T Ford. With quick glances to the sidewalks, she enjoyed seeing the dozens of shoppers as they hurried along the main street of downtown Milwaukee. The summer breeze threatened the brand new finger wave style of her flaming red hair. She was certain she looked at least twenty.

Jenny was startled when the police officer in the center of the intersection at Fifth Street blew his whistle for traffic to stop. The Ford was nearly halfway across so she continued forward. His arms waved while he tooted repeatedly and signaled for her to back up, then, eventually, gave the signal for her to pull forward. Her heart pounded as he walked toward her.

Jenny had mailed a quarter to the Motor Vehicle Department and received her license just days earlier. Her older brother, Art, took her out for a few driving lessons, so she was confident with her abilities. Pa thought she was too young to drive, so they had to sneak in the lessons while he was at work or napping.

Today, Ma allowed her to drive downtown to Gimbel's Department Store. Ma had picked out fabric to re-cover the davenport and finally talked Pa into the purchase. Since she wasn't sure of Jenny's driving abilities, luck was with Jenny when none of the older kids were around to do the errand. More luck was with her after Pa decided to drive up to Green Bay for a day or two with Uncle Mike.

When the officer approached the car, Jenny sat up straight and exuded confidence.

"Hi," she said cheerfully. She expected him to be dazzled with her new hairdo and second best dress. It was bright green and looked great with her hair.

The police officer was young and very good-looking, his hair as red as hers. He started to smile at her, then looked as though he just remembered he was an officer of the law and had to act with authority. He stood tall. "Didn't you hear me blow my whistle for you to stop?"

"Yes, Officer, I did." Jenny fluttered her eyelashes.

"You were supposed to back up. There was plenty of room."

"Well, you see," she hesitated and dropped her voice as she tapped her fingernails on the steering wheel, "I haven't been driving very long and I still haven't learned how to go in reverse."

He almost laughed when he said, "Let me see your license." He was obviously looking her over. Everything would be all right. She could feel it.

"What's your name, Officer?" she smiled up at him as she proudly handed him her new license.

"It's Flanagan, Miss."

"I'm Jenny Smith," she smiled and showed her dazzling white teeth.

While Flanagan looked at her license, Jenny watched his face change from a smile to a scowl. "Is this your license?"

"Yes," she added a giggle.

He handed back the license. All flirtation stopped. Without a word, he wrote a ticket and abruptly handed it to her. She was confused. Mentally, she kicked herself for not having worn the new dress with the bigger collar. It would have made her look more sophisticated.

Upset, Jenny started the car and pulled into traffic completely forgetting her errand. All she could think of was that Pa was going to kill her for getting a ticket much less driving without his permission.

She drove back to her neighborhood feeling depressed. Luckily, she had asked the police officer his name. She had an idea. Her friend, Eddie could help.

Eddie waved when he saw her pull in to the gas station where he worked. His lanky frame sauntered toward her. His overalls were grimy, and his fingernails were dark with grease.

"Hi, Jenny. What're you doing here?" He walked back and forth to check out the car. "Nice car. Does your Pa know you're driving it?" He laughed.

She ignored his question. "I'm here because I need to ask a favor. I just got a ticket, Eddie."

"So, what do you want me to do?"

"You know a lot of the cops, so this is what I want. Go buy a bottle of whiskey. I'll give you the money," she added quickly. "And, I want you to give it to the cop who gave me the ticket, so he'll tear it up. I know you've done this before for friends, and I'm a friend, aren't I?"

"What's his name?" Eddie asked, warily.

"It's Flanagan. He's tall and young and very good-looking." Jenny smiled at her recollection.

"Save your money," Eddie said flatly.

"What do you mean?" Jenny scowled.

"He won't tear up your ticket. Your real name is Schmidt not Smith, and no Flanagan will tear up a ticket for a Schmidt. Your license says Schmidt, doesn't it?"

"I don't understand. I grew up as Smith and Ma's Irish," Jenny tried to convince him.

"I know that, but he doesn't, and your Pa's name is Schmidt.

Eddie knew the story about her growing up in Montello, Wisconsin as Jenny Smith. Her family started using the name years before because of the animosities toward the Germans in WWI. It wasn't until their move to Milwaukee and Jenny registering at West Division High School that she needed her birth certificate. She learned then that her real name was Genevieve Schmidt.

"Flanagan's Pa was killed by the Germans during the war. You're lucky he didn't throw you in jail." Eddie laughed and walked back to the garage. "Pay the ticket," he yelled over his shoulder.

The next day Ma let her drive the Model T again to pay the ticket at the courthouse. It was $3.50, and Pa wasn't to know, which suited Jenny just fine. Art promised he'd show her how to go in reverse as soon as he had extra time, but she'd have to be very careful today.

The courthouse was located at the top of a steep hill. Jenny knew luck was with her when she found a parking spot facing downward. All she'd have to do is pull forward to leave.

After finding the place to pay the ticket, she stood in a long line. When Jenny went back to the Model T, she was horrified. While gone, a squad car had parked in front of it and she didn't know how to back up.

She sat in the Ford while looking up and down the street and waited for someone to come and move the squad car. It was time to get home. Pa was due and she needed to get moving.

Eventually, Jenny decided there was only one thing to do. She started the engine, shifted into first gear and let up on the clutch, then slowly moved the car forward. With a slight nudge to the squad car, she was sure to get out.

The car in front of her moved, as planned...and kept moving. Jenny pulled the Model T away from the curb, stepped on the gas and sped past the moving squad car just as it hit another car parked twenty feet down the hill.

Jenny was scared, but never looked back. The way her luck was running it was probably Flanagan's squad car. Her next objective was to learn how to put the Model T in reverse and learn it quick.

Genevieve Schmidt Harris is now ninety-nine years old and has never received another ticket. She still lives in Milwaukee and relinquished her driver's license at age ninety-one. She never forgot Officer Flanagan.

Justice Is Served
Glory Wade

Mark jolted to the buzzing in his ear, scraping the knuckles of his right hand against a rough cold surface where his alarm clock should have been. Pain spasmed down the length of his other arm and his hand convulsed against a dirty, cracked concrete floor. He cursed and his eyes sprang open to a cement wall dotted with dark splatters.

Odors of mold, urine, and feces, and something he could not identify, were overpowering. He squeezed the muscles of his nostrils to make them as small as possible.

Lying still, he focused on his surroundings. The incessant buzzing continued, constantly changing in volume. It emanated from his left shoulder, which felt wet and cold. A moving black shadow took flight and hovered as he turned his head to look. A familiar metallic odor defiled his nostrils. The droning shadow returned.

Fear rose in the man as he hesitantly moved his right hand to evaluate the wound, being as still as possible to minimize the pain. As his fingers neared the site, the buzzing in his ear became angry and he felt the rising of indignant black bodies. A shudder coursed through him. He knew they were flies. His shoulder was covered with a viscous substance. He knew it was his blood. Terror surged like bile through his body, lodging in his throat. He knew he wasn't dreaming.

With trembling hand, he moved his wet fingers to within his view. The dim light of early dawn filtering through the dirty pane of a window high in the opposite wall allowed him to see the crimson smear. Images of it dripping onto his abdomen and pooling out on the ground beside him sliced across his mind.

"Oh, god. I'm dying! I'm dying!"

Through the surreal fog clouding his thoughts, he heard a chorus of voices, "Remember what you did."

Mark breathed deeply, as deeply as he could without feeling excruciating pain, and he focused. In between swells of nausea, pieces of what had happened crept forward, gaining momentum until they flashed before him, a montage. Visions of walls blurring past him. Sirens and chasing feet. The pounding of his heart in his ears. The searing in his lungs. The slamming of a policeman's bullet into his shoulder. Slinking into the hidden entrance to an old tenement, finally finding refuge. Falling into a dank, dark corner of the basement. Then all had gone black.

The blackness made way for a little voice. It teased, "Remember what did you did."

The buzzing of the flies intensified and a black spider the size of a large tarantula stared at him from the middle of her lacework. He wondered how the web could hold her weight.

His eyes grew wide and his throat felt sand paper dry. Yes, he did remember, and he knew where he was. Images of innocent eyes wide with terror and distorted faces and broken limbs paraded before him, playing like a video in his mind. Terror replaced the thrill that he had always felt when he relived his "games". The spider moved closer fixing him with the intensity of her stare. Her eyes morphed into a kaleidoscope of the battered faces of his victims.

He turned his head at the sound of footsteps on the floor above. They seemed so far, far away but hope flickered.

"Please help me! Help me!" he begged. Flies flew into his open mouth, but no one came. No one with two legs.

A huge black rat scuttered across the cold floor onto his ribs. Razor-sharp claws pierced his chest and left shoulder, holding him hostage. The rodent's whiskers tickled his chin as its eyes gleamed directly into his. "Remember what you did."

One long accusatory look then the rat chomped a piece out of his shoulder. Horror and unbearable pain sliced through Mark.

The reverberation of hundreds of clicking feet thundered in his ears. He silently screamed as a squirming mass of heavy bodies with gnashing teeth covered his body. When he pushed at those near his right hand, it became hors d'oeuvres. The buzzing of the flies grew louder. Ants swarmed over him and clicking cockroaches scurried to join the feast.

He lay helpless, unable to fight back, unable to save himself. His body felt every violation and he prayed for death to come quickly.

The spider hovered closer and the man's victims smiled at him one by one. The final one loomed the largest, her face inches away. She was the girl child he had brought to this very basement a mere two days ago. One eye was swollen shut, her pale face bruised and broken as he had left her. Blood still clotted in her fair hair. She laughed and all of his victims floated behind her, pointing their fingers at him. He screamed and pleaded for death to release him. To no avail.

Justice is served.

My Life as a Sperm
W. Darrah Whitaker

Stacy walked into my hospital room the day after I died. She's a loyal assistant, not too bright, what do they say, not the sharpest tool in the shed, but she's nice to look at and she puts up with me, which says a lot for her patience. Gotta like that about her. I know that work never takes a day off in the show business game, even if you're in the hospital, and she plays along.

"Oh my god, Buddy, you look awful." That was the first thing out of her mouth when she entered. Not that it wasn't true. I'm sure I looked like shit. Who doesn't after getting rammed by a Tahoe going fifty? We just don't want to necessarily hear about it. What do they say, from the mouth of babes? And believe me, she was a babe. She wore a tight black skirt, the kind that makes it physically impossible not to swish while you walk. She liked wearing stuff that showed off her assets. No one was complaining from this side of the room.

"Thanks, Sweetcheeks. I got all dressed up just for you."

"Come on, Buddy. You're not dressed up at all."

She hung her oversized handbag on the back of a chair and sat down. She had already whipped out her pad and was ready for notetaking, just like I told her when I woke her up at five this morning. I had her trained well.

"One thing, Buddy." She did have the sweetest way of saying my name. Almost sounds like pudding. Her lips pout just the slightest as she says it. Pudding. "Mr. Zimmerman told me to let you rest, so you can't breathe a word of this to no one. Okay?"

"It'll be our little secret, Stace. Now, get that pencil ready 'cause I've got a lot I need to say."

And I did because not many people can say they died twice in one day.

"My name is Buddy Price and I died twice yesterday." I like to hit them with a good first line. Gotta hook them or you're toast. "The first time I died, I was told it was for two minutes and thirty-two seconds before they placed the paddles on my chest and zapped me back to life."

"You know, Stace, for thirteen years, I've worked in Hollywood for Zimmerman Talent, and in that time, I've brought in quite a few clients and, you know, gotten a bit of a reputation."

"Yeah," she chuckled, smacking her gum.

"It's funny how little reputation helps you when you're lying on a gurney in the back of an ambulance fighting L.A. traffic. It's at that point you realize that no one really gives a shit."

"No, that isn't true, Buddy. A lot of people care."

"See any flowers in the room, babe?"

"No, but it's early. No one knows what happened."

"Not for long." I tossed the Enquirer over onto her lap. I was front page news. "Look, we can have this little discussion later. Let me get back on track."

"Okay, I'm ready."

"The car that hit me came out of nowhere, T-boned me right in the intersection of Robertson and Santa Monica. Somebody famous must have been eating lunch at the Robertson Deli down the block because my bang attracted a bunch of paparazzi. I guess they figured they were gonna get their very own Princess Diana picture. You know, shot of a lifetime. I remember lying half in, half out of the car, with all these guys shouting at me. 'Look over here. Look over here.' Thank God it was my Beemer and not the Prius. It would have been a helluva mess. If I had felt like being environmentally friendly, I wouldn't be talking with you right now. That Prius would have crumpled like a tin can".

"What does that tell you about global warming?" I asked her.

"Global what?"

"Never mind. Anyway, I remember seeing this one guy who'd run the gauntlet and was hanging back a little, taking some shots. That's when I died the first time. Lights out. The next thing I know, I'm alive again and this asshole is standing right over the paramedic's shoulder snapping away. He got that picture of my eyes bugging out when they zapped me back to life. I should get commission."

She picked up the Enquirer and looked more closely at the cover. There I was, blood-caked hair framing eyes that truly looked like they were about to bust out of my head.

"Well, at least he got your good side."

"Jesus Christ, Stacy, there isn't any good side when you're dead."

"Yeah, I guess so," she said laying the paper back down.

"To tell you the truth, I was kind of disappointed when I died."

"How can you be disappointed if you're dead, Buddy?"

"You know, you're right, Stace." She gave me a big red-lipped smile. "Say that I was disappointed about the death experience. That sound good? See, there was no white light for me, no tunnel lined by relatives waving me on to the finish line. I hear people who've died say they get all warm and fuzzy; some don't even want to come back. All I got was darkness. Sounded a little like a cave, in fact."

"How do you know, Buddy?"

Writer's Bloc III

"Well, I yelled out a few times."

"Were you scared?"

"No, babe, I wasn't scared. I was just yelling out to see if anybody was around. It kind of sounded echoey. Like a cave. Well, not too long after ending up in there, they brought me back. Hurt like a motherfucker."

"I bet. You know one time I stuck my fingernail file in the electrical socket and that hurt sooooooo much," she said.

"Why in the world did you – never mind." Like I said, not the sharpest tool. "Let me finish this up, Stace. I'm gonna start forgetting things if you keep interrupting me."

"Okay, okay, go on." She raised her pencil, poised for more.

"Shit, now where was I?"

"You were in a car accident."

"Thanks for that."

"No problem," she said with this big smile, wiggling a little in her chair to get more comfortable.

"Okay, I'll tell you about the accident. I'm driving along talking on my cell with Ethel Silvers, that up and coming actress, you know, from "I was a Teenage Vampire". Beautiful as the day is long, legs all the way up to her ass, what can I say. We were talking about changing her name. No one's going to make it in this business with a name like Ethel."

"What about Ethel Merman?"

"Stacy, do you mind?"

"And Ethel Barrymore? Wasn't she somebody?"

"Stacy!"

"Sorry."

"Like I was saying, you're not going to make it in this town with an old lady name, I told her. No matter how gorgeous you are, people aren't going to see sexy with a name like Ethel. Well, I got hit out of nowhere. My Beemer was tough, but not tough enough to hold off a ton of Tahoe. Hit me broadside, right in the door. That's why my whole left side is so fucking broken. You know who the other driver was? ...Marty Schwartz."

"Marty? You're kidding. Small world, isn't it?" Marty was a guy at ICA who I butted heads over some projects, a real world-class asshole.

"I get it from a very reliable source that he was coked out of his mind. He went right through the windshield, probably sailed right over my head before hitting the pavement twenty feet down the street. He landed in the crosswalk right at the feet of Keanu Reeves. He bounced right up, gave Keanu his card, and collapsed right back down, dead."

"Come on, Buddy. How would you know that?"

"Just hold on, Stace. You'll understand as soon as I get there."

"Hopefully," she said tapping her pencil against her notebook.

"Okay, so I'm lost again. All right, so I died, I came back, and then they brought me here to Cedars. So the next thing I know I'm waking up with this doctor in the ER patching me up. He's telling me that my left arm is fractured in two places, my left leg, the tibia, broken, three of my ribs and I got a concussion. He says that I'm lucky to be alive. And I look over at this nurse who's helping out and I'm thinking, yeah, Doc, I am lucky to be alive. I wouldn't want to miss out on a sight like that. God, the casabas on her. Doc, ask her if she'll wave at me in my tunnel."

"Buddy, I hope you won't get mad. But I'm dying for a cigarette. Are we going to take a break or something soon?"

"Hang on, Stace. I'm just getting to the good stuff."

"Well, I hope so because I think you're just being gross right now."

"What can I say? I'm a sucker for a pretty face. You should know that."

"Yeah, I do," she said looking down at her notebook.

"Okay, you want the good stuff. Here it is. They all think

I'm out of the woods. They've set my leg, casted up my arm, pumped me up with some drugs that are doing wonders for the pain, let me tell you. And then I go and die again. One second, I'm looking at Miss Nurse Universe, and the next thing I know, it's dark again. I'm going, shit, not again. This is fucking ridiculous. But this time, things go differently. All of a sudden, I feel this intense pressure and then I'm moving like a million miles an hour, shooting up this tunnel towards a white light, and I'm feeling all warm and fuzzy. I don't see anybody waving at me, but I'm thinking, finally, at least if I'm dead, I'm not going to be sitting in a cave for the rest of my life."

"Funny."

"What's funny?"

"You said for the rest of your life. That's funny 'cause you're dead."

"Okay, okay, figure of speech. Change that if it makes you happy. Anyway, I'm shooting along thinking I'm going to God. And that's a stretch for me. I'll be the first to admit I wasn't the most religious guy growing up. My parents took me to church, but I think they did that because they didn't want to feel guilty, like they hadn't given me a chance with Him. But, later, over the years, I didn't go except when somebody either died or got married, what's the difference, you know. But, it looked like God was feeling merciful that day and I was going to make out okay. But slowly, I felt like I wasn't moving so fast anymore, it was kind of becoming a struggle to get to the light. I knew with every fiber of my being that I needed to get to that light, but it was getting so hard. At first, I was just flying along, but then I was feeling it, like I was running a marathon and my legs just didn't have any more juice."

"Well, you aren't really in the best shape, you know, Buddy."

"Yeah, I know. I know. But that doesn't have anything to do

with anything. Come on, Stace. Let me get this out. Anyway, so I've been staring at this white light, really concentrating on that when I look over and see I'm not the only one. There were a bunch of other guys swimming along with me."

"Swimming? You were swimming, Buddy?"

"Yeah, at that moment, I realized I was swimming. And one of the guys next to me is none other than Marty Schwartz. He's moving right along with me and he looks over and says, 'Sorry about hitting ya' Buddy.' Can you believe the nerve of that guy? He just killed me and all he can say is 'Sorry about hitting ya' Buddy.'"

"Yeah, well, with Marty, I can," she replied.

"And he goes on about how God's got this warped sense of humor because the one time he actually gets a chance to meet Keanu Reeves, he's lying dead on the pavement. That's how I know about Keanu. Marty told me. You know I sure as hell didn't see that myself."

"Well, you could have read it somewhere."

"I didn't read it, Stacy. I'm telling you, this really happened.

"Sure, Buddy."

"So, as we're getting closer to the light, I notice something's different about me. I'm not in my body at all."

"Well, that makes sense, since you're dead and all."

"Yeah, well, get this. I'm a sperm."

"A what?"

"A sperm. An honest-to-god, bona fide, Grade A sperm."

"Come on, Buddy. You're pulling my leg. Really?"

"As God is my witness and, Stace, I can really say that because God was my witness."

"You're sounding crazy, Buddy."

"I'm really a sperm and I see that Marty and I and this kid from Cleveland are the only ones left and we're doing all what we can to get to the white light. That white light, Stace, is God and he's holding this little egg in his hand. Well, it was actually pretty big compared to me, but in God's hand, it was pretty small. God's got some height."

"You were a sperm?"

"Yeah, a sperm. Now, just go with it."

"Yeah, I'll go with it, Buddy," she said, shaking her head.

"Well, anyway, he looks down at the three of us and says, 'Who of you are worthy of going back?' Marty, of course, pipes up immediately and says that he's the guy for the job. Just like Marty, trying to suck up to the Big Guy. How many clients has he tried to steal from us?"

"Lots," she said, not looking up.

"So Marty starts in on God, asking him about his robe, where he got it, that his sandals are looking very chic, schmoozing like only Marty can do. It's making me sick. But I keep my mouth shut, because it's God, you know, and I'm freaking out a little by this time. Here's God standing in front of me and I'm a frickin' sperm. Well, the guy to my right is a teenager from Cleveland. Don't ask me how I know, I just know by looking at him."

"How did you know?"

"Are you even listening to me? I said I just knew."

"Okay, Buddy. Don't bite my head off."

"Well, the kid is feeling kind of sad because he hadn't really gotten a fair break in his previous life. He died the night of his senior prom. Didn't even get a chance to get lucky with his date. Apparently, she puts out."

"You just know that, right, Buddy?"

"Right. Well, Marty finally finishes his spiel and then God turns to me. I'm thinking to myself, what angle can I play? Then I say, 'God, I know that I've made a bunch of mistakes in my life, I know I don't treat people right, I'm selfish, vain, and pretty much an asshole. Believe me, the seven deadly sins are sitting on the top shelf of my refrigerator at home. So, you know what, God, I'm going to take a pass.'"

"I tell him, 'Talk to the kid to my right, I think he deserves a second chance. I mean, he didn't even get a chance to get laid. The least you can do is throw him a bone.' God looked at me and smiled. Stacy, I've never seen a more beautiful smile in my life. It's like all your worries just slip away when you get a smile like that. And he says, 'I agree with you Buddy. The kid gets to start over. And, him,' he said glancing over his shoulder at Marty, 'well, him, not so much. But, you, I'm going to send back and you can pick up where you left off. On one condition.'"

"Well, I know right off I'm going to say okay. I worked the angle with God and it looked like it was going to pay off. And, boom, I get sent back and the next thing I know I'm staring up into the ceiling of the ER. That nurse is just hanging right over me, and I could just reach out and grab those melons, but I'm strapped down and all I can do is smile. I'm back, Stace, I'm back with blessings from God."

"That sounds pretty unbelievable."

"It's crazy, huh? But it really happened."

"So what was the condition? He said under one condition. What was it?" Stacy said edging up on her chair.

"He told me I had to change my life, be a better person. Not too many people get a second chance, he said, so make the best of it. You know, maybe go into a different line of work. Where you can make a difference, he said. How about that God for ya'?"

"So are you going to do it?"

"What do you mean, Stace? I am a changed man. Don't you see it?"

"Sure, Buddy. I see it."

"Okay, I want you to write that up. Let's get it into some kind of workable treatment. Send it over to the guy who wrote "Bruce Almighty", what's his name. He's with us, isn't he? Let him flesh it out to a feature script. At the very least, we get a TV movie. And remind me to get in touch with Keanu Reeves's agent. I think he'd be perfect to play me. And we need a title. How about "Godproof"? Write that down. Perfect title. Doesn't say too much, leaves them wondering. Or maybe "Tuesdays with God" 'cause this all happened on Tuesday."

"Okay, Buddy. Slow down. Are you sure you're okay? How's your head feeling?"

"Never felt better, Sweetcheeks. How many people can say they talked to God and he gave them a thumbs up? How many?"

"Not many."

"Life is going to be different for me now, Stace. You better believe it."

"Anything you say, Buddy."

"It's a whole new world, Stace. And one more thing. Remind me when I get back to the office to find out if God has an agent. I think He's ripe for a comeback."

First Encounter
(An Excerpt from her work in progress, a YA Novel, Freedom's Promise*)*
J. A. Wilkins

"P-Terous," Kar-Lynn called out to her ship, "Are you sure we're alone? Now that we've arrived, take another scan. See if that echo we heard a few hours ago still bounces back when you look behind us."

"I told you that echo faded two hours—twenty-one minutes ago," the feminine voice of her AI ship answered.

Kar-Lynn squeezed her eyes shut and pursed her lips. She sucked in a deep breath and allowed her irritation to pass with a slow exhale before she issued her order. "Just take one last scan of the system's perimeter. I have to make contact with the station and have them open the sensor corridor. If we are being followed, I don't want whoever may be out there listening in when I do."

"Oh, all right, if you insist, *my captain,*" P-Terous answered with an added touch of sarcasm. "I will perform the scan--again."

Kar-Lynn chewed on her bottom lip. *If I do nothing else when I get home,* she thought, *I will find out which of the jokers in maintenance tinkered with my ship's attitude.*

"I see nothing . . ." P-Terous' sentence faded away. "Well, well, well," she added after only a momentary pause, "I do believe there is someone out there. Something just brushed against my sensors at maximum range. It is hard to believe, but someone is trying to fool me!"

"Is it the same ship that followed us out of Tresdon Station last week?" Kar-Lynn asked.

"I *am* good, but I cannot perform miracles. I will have to wait until the contact comes within full range of my sensors to make an identification that detailed."

"Okay, P-Terous. You had better send out the distress call."

A new readout flashed across Kar-Lynn's Retinal display showing the prerecorded message P-Terous broadcast into near space. This message notified all ships passing within a parsec of Kar-Lynn's position that she had broken down and needed help. It also told those monitoring the ship from her home station that she was not alone and would not be coming in until she resolved the situation.

While she waited for a response from the other ship, Kar-Lynn made her way down to the engine room. Now, she must change out her perfectly good flow regulator valve with the worn and broken one she kept on hand for occasions like this.

Twenty minutes later, Kar-Lynn reentered the bridge. She held a nutriment bar in one hand, and the working regulator in the other. After placing the regulator at her station, she tapped her right temple twice to reinitiate her connection to P-Terous' external viewers. She blinked to allow the retinal implant in her left eye to adjust.

Kar-Lynn scanned the numbers running across the lower edge of the planet that hung in a holographic depiction on her optic nerve. She scanned the information on the readout while she checked the bank of switches along the back of the bridge's bulkhead.

She fought a frown and tightened her stomach against

her rising anxiety. *How could P-Terous and I have let someone tail me all the way here? Could her long talks with P-Terous have distracted her this much? Maybe, but it wouldn't have distracted her multitasking AI.*

She stared at the image of the unfriendly gas giant that hung in space where it had for a millennium. The red, yellow, and orange patterns and swirling eddies played across its surface. This beguiling spectacle, that dominated the system, fascinated and frightened the few seasoned pilots who navigated near it.

Not many ships stopped long enough to watch the brown and purple storms moving among its surface. Those ever changing, sometimes blending, hues of colors gave the planet its character. And unknown to those few, who did linger in this uninhabited system, was that one of those storms wasn't a storm at all. It hid the station that sheltered what remained of her captured civilization.

Kar-Lyn ignored the small corner of the planet's monstrous image displayed on her optic nerve. Her concentration remained on the stream of information sliding across the bottom of the flowing backdrop. At the corner of her perception lay the largest, darkest stain in the atmosphere of the gas giant. That Purplish-black blemish grew in depth every year. Had this system been populated, this growing disfigurement would cause a great deal of concern to its neighbors.

Despite the urgency of her work, she smiled. What travelers through this system did not know was that this blemish hid her people from their enemies, the Thrallers. That expanding blot, swirling in the planet's upper atmosphere, concealed her home, Ban-Orel. Until they recovered more of their citizens from the slavery thrust upon them by these marauders, her people must stay hidden from everyone in this sector of space—including whoever followed her.

"Still no word from that other ship?"

"I told you three point eight minutes ago that no message has been received. But the ship is on an intercept course. It is moving a little more cautiously than normal. But then, there is no accounting for the erratic actions of bio-life forms."

"Thanks P-Terous," Kar-Lynn muttered a hairs-breadth above a whisper.

"Present company excepted," P-Terous apologized. "I sometimes forget that you are a bio."

Kar-Lynn walked toward her console, knowing that AI ships never forgot anything. She placed her meal next to the touch pad console and picked up the working regulator. Stretching up, onto her toes, she reached behind the dormant, clear plexi-plate computer panel. At the tip of her reach, she laid her little finger on a small dot that resembled a stain on the bulkhead. When four faint lines appeared on the seamless wall, a cover plate slid open. It exposed a shelf just large enough for the regulator to rest on.

After depositing the unit and closing her hiding place, Kar-Lyn withdrew her arm. She stopped to check her reflection in the dormant panel. Her bright green eyes lit with amusement when she dabbed at a deliberately placed smudge on her cheek.

I know you are a young bio-life form." P-Terous' voice came from all around her. "But, must you wear your food on your face and clothing in the process of nourishing your body?"

"At seventeen, I may be the youngest pilot from home," Kar-Lynn told her ship, "but check your sensors, its grease. If we are broken down—and I am supposed to be working on fixing you—I would get dirty in the process. Wouldn't I?"

"Ah!" P-Terous conceded, "Point taken. Wait, I am receiving a message from the other ship."

"Put it through! Run it over the comm for me."

". . . And if you don't answer me, now," an angry male

voice echoed across the bridge, "I'll blow you to space dust. I repeat. Identify yourself. Send me your homeport ID and registration. And if you--"

"Well," Kar-Lynn interrupted his retort, "I must say--you have a charming introduction. Is this how you greet everyone you come across? Or do you save this tirade for those broken down and in need of help?"

"You sound young . . . but I have no time for slavers," the angry fellow continued. "So tell me if you're part of the Thrallers' network or one of their paid operatives. If you are, I'll leave, and you can pull in some other unsuspecting fool."

"And what makes you think I'd tell you if I were part of the slaver's network?" Kar-Lynn asked. She let her hands and eyes slide across the plexi-glass touching the faint lines of inactive squares etched upon it. She brought up a list of files. Opening one of them, she checked P-Terous' weapons. She also reached down onto her leg and pulled her sidearm from its holster. "I could tell you I wasn't and wait for you to come aboard and pounce on you."

"If you look anything like you sound, that may not be such a bad prospect. Now transmit your registry, and we can get on with getting acquainted."

Kar-Lynn frowned at his brashness. She signaled P-Terous to transmit the registry information intentionally omitted from the original message.

Why was this pilot out here? Had he followed her? Why hadn't P-Terous detected him until she prepared their link with the sensor network leading to her home?

"Is that better?" Kar-Lynn asked after P-Terous transmitted her forged merchant registry.

She relaxed, knowing that the registry identified her as Keri Lehman. It listed her family as freelance merchanters out of Stanley's Port, a small, sparsely populated world holding a tenuous treaty with the slavers. Stanley's Port felt safe helping her people because their planet held too little profit for the slavers to bother with.

"I must have forgotten to encrypt that information into my distress call in my rush putting it together. Please, accept my apologies for not identifying myself properly."

"Okay . . . uh, Lehman." The long pause that followed sent a shiver of foreboding through her. "Mind if I come aboard?"

"Sure," Kar-Lynn said while she rechecked the information downloaded at their first contact. "Your info looks legit. I guess we can trust each other. Are you going to link up, or come over by EVA?"

"Actually I thought I would dock my ship in your cargo bay . . . if it'll fit. Then, if it really is your power flow regulator that's gone out, we can replace it with mine. We can travel back to Tresdon Station for the replacement. I think you'll agree it's the closest colony where a reasonable replacement can be found. That is, unless there's some reason you want to sit out here by yourself until I return with the part."

After agreeing to take him aboard, Kar-Lynn cut the connection. "P-Terous, make preparations for our guest, and remember you must remain silent while he's aboard."

"Pleeeease! Give me some credit. Computers only think—AI's have the power of deduction."

After an hour of maneuvering the smaller ship into her cargo hold, Kar-Lynn hesitated, but finally whispered to P-Terous, "Initiate gravity inside the hold." She held her hand over the contact until her magnetic boots released their grip on the deck. When she let her hand pass over the contact, the hatch that separated the hold from the rest of the ship opened. She watched the brash fellow from the intercom strut across the floor. He didn't look dangerous, but she had stopped judging people by their looks during her internship on Par-Shan's ship.

The young man, not much older than herself, held out his hand when he arrived at her side. "My name is Tory Ansel. I am sorry about my angry attitude when I spoke to you over the comm, but when you didn't answer--well, you know how it is with all the slavers ships about." He stuck his hand out further. "I am pleased you are not in league with them?"

Kar-Lynn ignored the offered hand and turned to lead the way to her engine room. "It shouldn't take us more than an hour to remove my regulator and adapt yours into its place."

With their task finished, they entered the bridge, and Kar-Lynn set the controls for Tresdon Station. "I've put the ship on one-quarter speed to reduce the stress on our makeshift repair," she told him. She figured it would keep them close to her people longer—until she figured out this stranger's motives.

"Which colony did you say you were from?" Tory asked Kar-Lynn from a seat he had taken across the bridge.

She tapped her temple to cut off the RD implant and waited until her senses adjusted to the brighter light inside the ship. "My family runs our business out of Stanley's Port," she reminded him. Turning to face him she asked, "Why?"

"Oh," Tory continued, "it's just that I spent a good deal of time on Stanley's Port, and I think I would have remembered you." he said, his curious look taking in everything on the bridge.

Kar-Lynn checked the time until they left the system. *Five minutes and I'll be on my own.* "I'm a new freelancer. Remember?" She turned ever so slightly so he would not see her tap her temple to restart the implant in her eye. "This is my first solo trip, and I was just delivering this ship back home. Since I interned on one of our other ships for the last three years, I didn't spend much time docked on my home world. So I'm not surprised you haven't seen me around there."

Writer's Bloc III

Something in Tory's easy demeanor calmed Kar-Lynn's fears within a short time. She still wasn't sure about him, but his easy personality definitely grew on her. The more conversation he made, the more accustomed she became to the sound of his voice. She found it took greater and greater difficulty keeping her attention on their progress away from Ban-Orel. So, she allowed him to drone on with his brand of chit-chat, because she found she liked listening to his voice. His presence took her mind off how much she missed her comrades from the other ship.

Tory spewed one question after another at Kar-Lynn. At the appropriate times, she nodded and gave the usual uh-huhs while she concentrated on navigating the ship.

"What planets have you done business with?" he asked.

"Not many, yet," she admitted. "Bur our company does business with all thirteen of the open planets in the sector."

"Well, what kinds of cargo do you usually carry?"

Kar-Lynn glanced at him over her shoulder. "We ferry and sell a lot of things. We don't like doing business with the thrallers, so we are very selective in the cargo we haul." Without actually saying so, she hoped he understand how well they avoided the two planets control by them. "Primarily, I'm scheduled to transport ice from frozen worlds to planets in need of water and fuel. We have hauled raw ore and minerals from one world to the other, too."

"I just wondered how and why you become a freelance merchanter at such a young age."

"I become a freelancer out of necessity, but I'm not a full-fledged merchanter yet. I just finished my internship and, like I said before, I needed to bring this free ship home. It would have been an easy trip if I hadn't broken down."

While they talked, Kar-Lynn allowed the RD to deposit the ship's view of space onto her optic nerve without the aid of the screen. She stayed alert for anything out of the ordinary. Thinking her home world had sent out an escort, she watched one certain anomaly behind them in particular. When no contact came through P-Terous from the other ship, she forgot to answer Tory's questions. She concentrated greater interest on identifying what she saw.

From the corner of her eye she saw Tory start pacing the bridge. He stopped, placed his knuckles on his hips, and asked, "Am I boring you?"

"For the last few minutes," Kar-Lynn told him, unconsciously squinting at the image of the stars she saw through the RD, "someone out there has been following us."

"We're being followed? How do you know? Who is it?"

"I interned as navigator on one of our other ships and I still have a retinal implant."

"Don't you have any better more extensive sensors?"

Kar-Lyn smiled at his ignorance of the more advanced instrument. "There is nothing wrong with my equipment, but I can put it on the viewer if you want to see it."

Tory continued to question her while Kar-Lynn focused the holo-image on the screen before her. P-Terous aimed the sensors at the object for Tory's benefit while she concentrated on the information streaming across the bottom of holo-image. That far off ship mingled with the stars on the clear screen before them soon stood out on its own.

Kar-Lynn spun around to face Tory who stood just behind her, "Is there any reason you wouldn't want a face to face with a slaver patrol ship?"

She watched the hard muscles of his tall, lanky frame ripple in what looked like fear. His face took on a hard look of determination when he reached up and grabbed the collar of his jacket. Pulling hard at the magnetic fasteners, he ripped it open far enough for his shoulder to lie exposed. There, just below his left collarbone, he wore their mark.

The slaver's purple tattoo—that five star constellation stared back at her.

Writer's Bloc III

· · ·
  ·
 ·

She knew the rumor that the constellation, called The Watcher, depicted the stellar position of the slavers long ago destroyed home world. She learned long ago that the three stars running vertically represented an ancient mariner's body. The two stars jetting out in a swooping line, from just below the top star, formed the Mariner's arm. In the artistic depiction of the formation, the Mariner held an ancient spyglass.

It was rumored that the slavers altered that tattoo to resemble the view of that particular constellation from the spatial sector where they captured the slave. That way the slavers identified where their property came from at a glance. The largest star in the tattoo represented the elbow of the watcher and it identified the position in the constellation of the slavers ancient home.

"Did you escape?"

He gave her a curt nod.

"You want to be a slave again?"

He shook his head.

"Then we may have to sacrifice your ship. They will already have detected the refined metals in my cargo hold."

"It's okay." He shrugged, flashing a broad smile. "It's stolen, anyway."

"P-Terous," Kar-Lynn stated as she turned back to her instrument panel. "Guide our guest to the hiding place."

"Okay, Sir. If you will exit the bridge," P-Terous began, "and follow my directions. We will tuck you away where no one will ever find you. That is, unless we want them to."

"AI?" Tory asked, looking for the source of the voice.

"Of course I am," P-Terous answered before Kar-Lynn could open her mouth. "How else could a lone person run a ship this size?"

"Thanks, P-Terous," Kar-Lynn said, looking over her shoulder at Tory. "I think I'll try it on my own next trip."

Tory had not moved. He stared at Kar-Lynn. When she cocked her head at him, he turned and left the bridge.

"P-Terous, is it? Show me the way to this hiding place."

"Our guest is on his way," P-Terous advised Kar-Lynn. "Shall I cleanse his bio signature from both ships?"

"No, leave his signature on the scout ship. At least it will give them a trail to follow. Hopefully it will lead them away from us. And, P-Terous, don't forget to wipe all the communications to and from Tory's ship from your log."

"Again, I reiterate, give me some credit," came the ships lofty retort.

Some time later, after Kar-Lynn had replaced her broken regulator for the jerry-rigged one from Tory's scout ship, but before P-Terous had completely cleansed his bio-signature, the slavers scout ship came along side. The swiftness of their approach made her heart race. During her internship, her friends and she had managed to outwit them for the last three years, but now she balked at a solo, face-to-face meeting with them.

When the hail from the slaver's ship came, she didn't respond right away. "P-Terous," she addressed her ship instead, "are we ready for them?"

"No! Do we have no choice? I will continue erasing your guest's presence, and make sure I stay ahead of them. It is the best I can offer."

"Remember, P-Terous, you will have to function silent again—like a normal computer.

"You don't have to remind me," P-Terous said, in a very good imitation of irritated human. "I wouldn't talk to slavers if my pathways depended on it."

Kar-Lynn winced against the tightness building in her

chest. She did find herself smiling at the way P-Terous spit the word "slavers" out as though she actually felt real hatred for them.

"Thanks, P-Terous." She passed her hand over the comm. Contact. "Unidentified ship," she began her hail, "I am having engine difficulties. Can you render assistance? Do you have parts I could buy or barter for?"

"Transmit you registry!" came the brisk reply.

"Is that you Splain?" she asked. "It's me, Kari Lehman. I'm the new captain of the P-Terous. Are you going to show your teeth to a friend?"

"Confirmed!" came Splain's stiff reply.

"My, my, aren't we formal today?" she said against the flutters that filled her stomach. "You must have a big shot aboard?"

"You will keep to business, Lehman. I have no time for your feeble attempts at familiarity this day."

Kar-Lynn smiled to herself. "Same as always, huh? One of these days I'll wear you down and get a friendly response out of you."

"I greatly doubt that. Now, prepare to link. And have your passenger stand by the ship in your hold."

"I have no passenger. The ship I'm ferrying is a derelict I found adrift."

"We will see. Prepare to be searched."

During the next thirty minutes one set of slavers confiscated Tory's stolen ship and removed it from her hold. Another team performed a full search of the P-Terous, or so they thought. Now, most of the slavers headed back to their patrol ship.

"Hey," Kar-Lynn shouted at the departing squad leader, "what about my compensation? The trade agreement you have with my home world says you'll compensate me for any legitimate material you confiscate. I found that derelict, and if it is stolen, like Splain said, then I am entitled to the reward. If not, then I could have sold it for salvage. So, either way you owe me compensation."

With her knees shaking, Kar-Lynn stood her ground, locked in a staring contest with the slaver towering over her. She knew if she relented she would loose the respect she had worked so hard to establish.

The tall, heavily armored slaver returned her glare. Without warning, his face split into a sadistic grin. He exchanged a glance over his shoulder at his comrades left on the bridge.

"Even with all I have heard about you, Lehman, I could kill you where you stand and rid us this day of your insolence. But you are young, and we should allow you time to learn. Beware, thought, that you do not overstep your bounds."

Kar-Lynn held her ground. Her eyes never wavering from the battle gnarled face of the squad leader.

The slaver reached for his belt. With a sudden jerk, that Kar-Lynn steeled herself against, he detached a small pouch and tossed it across the deck.

"Beware that one day you do not step across the brink, Lehman. But, I petition all our higher powers that I will be there to take care of you myself, when you do."

The squad leader bowed ever so slightly and Kar-Lynn's stomach turned when she caught the glint of admiration in his eyes. He turned and headed off the bridge. She didn't take a full breath into her lungs until he led the rest of his squad back through the link. She faced her console and monitored the detachment between P-Terous and the slaver's ship.

With the other ship on its way, she called out to Paterous, "Let Tory out!"

By the time Tory reentered the bridge, Kar-Lynn had made herself comfortable and allowed her head to relax against the headrest of her chair. She had also taken the precaution of resting her weapon on her lap.

"Tell me," she asked when Tory bent over to retrieve the money pouch from the floor, "how did they know I carried your ship in my hold?"

"I don't know. I told you—I stole that ship. I have no idea how they would know what you carry in your hold."

"I could have accepted that they would be curious over the extra refined metals they discovered when they scanned my ship, but they knew it was another ship before they arrived and demanded to see my passenger. *And*, their search just now was no more extensive than their normally curious look."

Kar-Lynn pointed her weapon at Tory. With practiced ease, she engaged the power unit with her little finger and allowed her thumb to hover over the contact.

"Now, let's start over," she said, a stern hardness filling her voice. "I want to know your true planet of origin, your real name, and how you supposedly escaped from the slavers."

Emily's Big Day
Brian T. Yates

Crossing the street from Margaritaville, the bride entered O'Shea's Casino on the Las Vegas Strip. She wore her wedding dress and only carried a small purse. There was no groom, no maid of honor or bridesmaids with her. People in the casino gave her passing glances as she walked past the table games and took a seat at the Dublin Up Bar.

The bartender's eyes widened when she sat in front of him. "What can I get you?"

"Absolute Vodka tonic with a lime."

He poured the drink and Emily downed it with a gulp. She pointed to the glass.

The bartender poured another round. "You want to run a tab?"

Money—it's always about money. Everyone wanted it and this bartender was no exception. Emily reached into her purse and pulled out a hundred dollar bill.

She sighed and stared into her drink. Today was supposed to be the happiest day of her life. Daddy rented an outdoor chapel at the Flamingo and brought Father Joseph to perform the ceremony. The ivory colored satin wedding dress made her the perfect bride. A hundred guests waited for her at the ceremony with three hundred more ready to attend a catered reception. Her parents had paid her one last visit to see her in her wedding dress. Tears rolled down Mom's face. She always cried at weddings.

While the bridesmaids and her maid of honor changed, the text message arrived. When she read it, Emily grabbed her purse and slipped away.

She looked around O'Shea's. It was a little hole in the wall along the Strip. The dealers seemed laid back as they laughed and talked with the guests. A pit boss sang a corny rendition of "Happy Birthday" to a woman turning beet red with embarrassment. Emily smiled. That turned into a big mistake.

A confident looking man with a sympathetic grin leaned on the bar and said to her, "Bad night, huh?"

"If you only knew."

"Tell me about it."

"Some other time."

Bachelor number two tried his luck and asked with a drunken slur, "Did the limo break down?"

She rolled her eyes at him. At least he was smart enough to leave.

Along came bachelor number three. "I didn't have any luck at the chapel either."

"Then keep trying."

Her cell phone buzzed. It was Brandy, her maid of honor.

Emily took a deep breath and calmly answered, "Hello."

"Everyone's looking for you. Where did you go?"

"Tell them I'm not coming back." She ended the call.

The text messages arrived one after another. Every bridesmaid and family member wanted to find her. Emily turned off her phone.

She wasn't going back. Let everyone be disappointed. It was only money. Emily thought about staying in Las Vegas. She'd serve drinks. From what she saw, the cocktail waitresses at O'Shea's got tipped most of the time. It looked like a reasonable living.

"What's that beautiful dress doing in a place like this?"

Emily's eyes opened wide. She turned her head and there stood Daddy in his tux. How on earth did he find her? No one knew where she went. No one in the wedding party saw her leave the Flamingo. Her father, Richard Moretti, sat next to her and ordered a beer.

Daddy made a phone call from his cell. "I found her." He nodded. "Yes dear, she's fine." He glanced at Emily. "Rather not say." Daddy smiled and shook his head. "Tell them to wait. If we're not back in time, then have the reception without us. We paid for the room and the entertainment. Don't let it go to waste." He ended the call.

"Mom?"

"Yep."

"She pissed?"

"Yep. Sophie and Marty are ready to leave."

They were Marco's parents and her potential in-laws. Neither liked the idea of coming to Las Vegas. They wanted a traditional ceremony back in Wellesley and the Tambroni's were the kind of people who got what they wanted.

Emily sighed. If her father told her to go back to the Flamingo and get married, she'd do it. Forget the text message. Forget the doubts and everything else. The problem was that both families were old school Catholics and once married, always married until death do us part. There'd be no divorce after today. Everything in her heart told her to stay away from the ceremony.

"Kind of hard to have a wedding with just one person," her father said.

Emily took a deep breath. "I'm pregnant."

"Then you shouldn't be drinking."

"I'm stressed."

Daddy glanced at her. "Does Mike know about your situation?"

Emily froze. Mike Risotto was Marco's best man. No one knew about their relationship. Emily and Mike kept their trysts private. None of her girlfriends knew because they'd talk. Mike had sworn his silence. It started out with a friendly drink. They visited the Gardner Museum in Boston. A dinner rendezvous led to a few hotel visits.

Tears rolled down her face. According to both families, particularly Sophie Tambroni, Emily and Marco were a match made in heaven and nobody disrespected the Tambroni's. The marriage helped solidify a business relationship between her father and future father-in-law.

Marco wasn't a bad guy. They dated in high school. She went to Boston College to study art while he attended Tufts for business. Their families were partners in the concrete business and had made a fortune with the Boston Big Dig and other projects around the city. Marco joined Sandstone Concrete after graduating and was being groomed to take over the company.

"Please don't tell," she begged her father. What was one more family secret?

Daddy remained stoic. A steely resolve came to his face. "If Mike's the father, you should marry him. After all, we're in Vegas, you two can elope."

"I didn't want to embarrass the family."

"Then why are you marrying Marco?"

That was a question she had spent the last few weeks pondering. A good many tears passed on that subject, particularly when the pregnancy test came back positive. Emily planned on having the child and calling Marco the father.

"I can't go through with this," Emily said.

Daddy took a drink. "I'm afraid things have changed."

"Because of me?"

He hesitated before answering, "I guess you haven't heard the news. The politicians back in Boston just issued an announcement concerning Sandstone Concrete."

Emily knew. That was the text message Mike sent her. The news ruined her family and everyone associated with Sandstone Concrete. The Big Dig was supposed to cost four billion dollars. Fourteen billion dollars later, the completed project turned into a huge boondoggle. The politicians in Boston and Washington demanded answers.

A Beacon Hill subcommittee audited Sandstone Concrete and learned the company used inferior materials in the construction. Parts of Route 95 and the Ted Williams Tunnel had to be rebuilt.

Emily looked at her father and saw fear in his eyes. He needed this marriage to take place. Marty Tambroni could protect him from the politicians. If Emily backed out of the ceremony, there'd be hell to pay. The two stared at each other until Daddy reached into his pocket. Pulling out a thick wad of bills, he put the money on the table.

"This will take care of you and Mike for a while. I'll put make a deposit into your bank account when I get home."

"You mean when we get home."

"No, when I get home because you and Mike are staying here. There's plenty of work in this town. Go to a casino off the Strip. Start small. Take any job they offer and work your way up. Whatever you do, don't come back to Boston."

"What about the Tambroni's?"

"I'll deal with them."

She took her father by the arm. "I don't want you to leave. Start a new life with us."

He ran his hand along her cheek. "I have to go back. When the time is right, I'll find you."

Emily watched her father leave O'Shea's and vanish into the passing crowd.

2009 Youth Contest Winner

Editor's note:

The HWG sponsors a youth writer's contest every year. Although we tried to contact previous winners, with no luck, we have included this years fiction winner. In our next edition, in 2012, we hope to include those who were omitted from this edition.

31 Days
Ariel Belanger

"How long have we been fighting this war again?"

Drew's words broke the silence that had filled the Sanctuary, muttered between chapped lips and a lit cigarette. His green-colored eyes sailed over the other two survivors that were spread out around the gun store, one peering through the cracks between the boards nailed over the windows, while the other caught up on the sleep she'd missed over the past few days.

Roger—an African-American of thirty-three whose size couldn't hide the fear in his eyes—took his gaze off the dead streets of New York and looked at Drew. He frowned. "What the hell kind of question is that?"

"Just wondering," Drew said, leaning forward in his chair. The twenty-five year old fingered the sniper rifle that lay against the wall beside him. "It just seems like forever since we all first met in that military truck that was supposed to take us out of the city and to some sort of safety in Boston. Instead...you know...it was overrun by the Infected, which led to it crashing and us having to make our own way through this hellhole to a 'security' that might not even exist anymore. I mean, how much farther are we from the city limits? Still, like, three days when it comes to walkin'-"

"Thirty-one days."

Drew paused. "Pardon? Thirty-one days until we're out of New York City?"

Roger shook his head. "No. It's been thirty-one days since we first met."

"Hot damn. And we're still not out of New York?" Drew chuckled. "We're pathetic."

As Roger sighed, returning his attention to the outside world, their companion, no older than sixteen, stepped forward toward Drew. "Got an extra cigarette?" she asked, blue eyes stern.

Drew eyed her, flashing a smirk. "Samantha, I thought I told you you're too young to be smoking."

"Shut up," Samantha muttered, grabbing a cigarette from the box Drew had offered despite his remark. "You're not my father, you know. My father's probably already dead anyway."

Drew's lips twitched. "That's right...your parents were forced to evacuate on a different truck?"

"Yeah." Samantha blew out a ring of smoke, watching it hover toward the ceiling and disperse. "And I haven't heard from them since. That means they're either phone-less, or they're dead."

"You don't seem to be too worried for the latter."

"Because I don't give a damn about them."

Drew blinked. Even Roger had looked over at that.

Samantha met Roger's eyes. Her voice was firm, serious, and it lacked a sense of sorrow, but still sounded bothered all the same. "Stop looking at me like that. To my parents, I was a burden. Despite that I got good grades and practically did crap that would forge my name on the gates to heaven, my parents rarely gave me a glance." She blew out another ring of smoke. "So, I was put into an environment where I had to literally fend for myself."

"Sounds tough," Drew said, sarcasm no longer riding his tone. "You're quite mature for your age. Most teenage girls in your position would be whining and crying on how adults never understood what it was like being young."

Samantha snorted. "Well, you'd be amazed how fast kids grow up when their parents don't baby them twenty-four-and-seven."

Drew looked at Roger, who had gone back to staring out the boarded window. His smirk returned. "What about you, Roger? What's your story? How was your life before that government experiment broke out and turned most of the world's population into man-eating zombies?"

Roger sighed, reloading his gun. "I ran a flower shop towards the eastern side of the city-"

"Wow...I admit I didn't see that one coming," Drew cut in, eyeing Roger's bulky figure.

Roger glared. "Don't interrupt me. Anyway, I ran a flower shop that was small—as in, it didn't get a lot of business year-round, but it was still a place I enjoyed working at. My mother and father are all the way up in Maine, so I have no idea if they're even alive. But, the thing is, I grew up in a garden, or at least always close to one. My mother was a heavy gardener. She would always be growing things in our backyard. When I moved out and on my own, I continued the tradition." Roger frowned. "I have to admit, I would prefer to be growing roses right now then shooting zombies in the head with a shotgun."

Drew switched his eyes between Samantha and Roger, not even acknowledging the scraping sound of an Infected dragging its claws against the door from outside. He ran a hand through his blonde hair. "Well, I suppose it's my turn, right?"

Silence.

"Thanks for sounding interested, guys. Anyway, I was born in Vegas. Weird, right? I'm scrawny. I look like a nerd. Everyone I've ever met assumed I was born in, like, Chicago or something, but not a risky place like Sin City." Drew leaned back in his chair, grinning. "When I still lived in Vegas, I practically gambled away every single penny I earned, which pissed my parents off beyond belief. It went as far as to where they were disappointed in me, and it was something like that, that made me realize that risking everything I had to get money was not what was going to make my parents proud of me. So...I moved here to New York a few years ago to attend college to become a doctor. Of course, all of my teachers became Infected before they finished teaching me my ABCs, but that's beside the point."

Samantha looked at him, eyes narrowed. "Why does your back story surprise me more than Roger's?"

"Don't know, darlin'. Perhaps I'm highly unpredictable. Vegas does that to you."

As Samantha rolled her eyes, Drew looked at Roger. "Hey," he said, "isn't it weird?"

"What?" Roger asked, arching a brow.

"How we're all different at first. I mean, Sam hates her parents, you don't talk to your parents enough, and I was willing to completely change my lifestyle just to get my parents to smile at me." Drew cocked his head. "But, at the same time, we're all kind of...similar? We're all people who are expected to have certain attitudes, but instead have attitudes that completely contradict the attitudes we're expected to have."

Samantha met Roger's eyes.

"And now we're all stuck in this hellhole of a town," Drew continued, "and we're fighting a zombie apocalypse while trying to find a place where we can stand still for more than one hour. We're like a crazy family just by ourselves."

Roger remained silent, but Samantha eventually looked at Drew, her frown not as tight as it was before. "Well," she muttered, "maybe if I had you two for big brothers, then I wouldn't feel so..."

"Alone?" Drew offered.

"…sure, let's just say that."

Drew smirked. "Love ya too, Sam."

Samantha rolled her eyes and grabbed her machetes. Meanwhile, Roger hooked his bullet belts across his torso and readied his combat rifle.

"We better get moving," he said.

Drew sighed. "Already? I thought we were just in the midst of a friendshippy moment."

Roger ignored him, beginning to unlatch the multiple locks holding the front door in place.

Drew, holding his sniper rifle, looked over at Samantha as they both waited to charge outside. "Ready to try to survive for the next few hours?"

Samantha met his eyes. "As long as you and Roger do the same and not get yourselves killed."

"Aw, you care. It's amazing what kind of crap can bring people together," Drew said, flashing her a cheesy smile.

Smiling back for the first time, Samantha watched as Roger slowly opened the door to the outside world. "Yes, it is."

The three survivors moved forward toward the horde of Infected that had gathered on the street, their guns ready.

Thirty-one days ago they came together as strangers to fight for their survival.

And thirty-one days later, they fought together as a family.

Contributors

AUTHOR CONTRIBUTORS
(In Alphabetical Order)

Grace Andrews
Grace Andrews grew up in the mountains of southern Oregon and has lived in several states in the U.S. and Europe. One of one hundred world-wide students, she was accepted into the Maui School of Writers in 1997. A novelist, Grace is working on a five volume saga. Recently catching the poetry bug, she is an active participant in Laudably Tarnished, a poetry workshop, a member of Sisters in Crime, Vegas Writers, and past Treasurer of the Henderson Writers Group, sponsor of the Las Vegas Writers' Conference. Grace has published articles in newspapers and the Fibromyalgia Newsletter. More of a thinker than a talker, writing gives Grace an avenue for the expressions of her inner self, allowing more freedom to explore thoughts and feelings. "Without this freedom," says Grace, "there is nothing."

Alba Arango
Alba Arango is a secondary school teacher of eighteen years. With Bachelor's degrees in both Education and History as well as a Masters degree in American History, Alba enjoys the telling of a good story and has decided to turn her attention and talents to the writing of middle grade fiction and short stories. Her first short story, *Vampires in Vegas*, was published online by the Las Vegas Review Journal. *Murder in Hadbury Manor* is her first

short story to be published in print. Alba just completed her first middle grade fiction book, *The Magic Sapphire*, which tells the exciting adventure of three twelve-year-old detectives and the mystery they encounter when they decide to search for a hidden treasure called the Magic Sapphire

Paul Atreides

Paul Atreides is a Civil Engineering Designer and lives in Las Vegas. Me, My Dad & Josh is his first attempt at fiction. Other works include the short stories Rosilies Best Christmas and Heirlooms of Misfortune. His first play, Phallusies, is scheduled for production this summer and he is currently working on his first book Ghosts (working title), a humorous work of fiction.

Darlien C. Breeze

Darlien is the author of MINI TALES, short mysteries for busy people. A California native, she is a sixteen year resident of Las Vegas. Her grandfather was a copper and gold miner. As a child she learned to sort mine rubble into mineral-bearing ore versus plain rock. The town was Cross Roads, 30 miles of unpaved, washboard roads away. We had no electricity and hauled water from the Colorado River. Fresh meat was rabbits and quail krilled from our cabin window by my crack-shot grandmother's .22. She taught school for 17 ½ years, sold real estate, owned and operated an import/export business, and am currently a vocational counselor. Other books: *Small Pony*, the story of a Navajo boy who has to decide between his world and the white man's. (volume in library systems of Los Angeles, Long Beach, and Riverside California). She wrote *Import/Export And You* as a textbook for classes, and taught at the Community College of Southern Nevada. *Ghosts &*

Contributors

Gamblers and *A Life of Crime* are scheduled to come out this year.

Garry Buzick

Garry Buzick lives in Las Vegas, recently relocating from the mountains of Colorado. He is a member of the Henderson Writer's Group and participates in the Laudably Tarnished Poetry Workshops. He is currently compiling a collection of poems, quotes and rants, Pain, Pleasure and Pandoras'. He has two novels awaiting publication: *Visitant*, a fast paced paranormal psychological thriller and *Throwaways—Perfect Match*, a paranormal thriller skewered with comedic bloody relief. Contact at: buzickg@yahoo.com

A.L. Campbell

Audrey Balzart (writing as A.L. Campbell) is an active member of the Henderson Writers' Group and a retired USAF Communications Planner. Audrey writes Young Adult, Action-Adventure, and Sci-Fi. Her AJ Silver MisAdventure series combines all three. She is the Conference Coordinator for the 2010 and 2011 Las Vegas Writers Conferences.

Alejandro E. Czeisler

Born in Buenos Aires, Argentina, from European immigrants, Alejandro Esteban Czeisler was raised in his family's traveling show, "Circus Tihany" which toured throughout the Americas. He moved with his parents to the Sarasota, Florida at age 16, graduated from Riverview High School and received his Bachelor's degree from Johnson & Wales University. In his writings, Alejandro explores the behind-the-scenes world of the circus and its travels as well as his European roots and immigrant experience.

Douglas A. Davy

Douglas was born August 7, 1948, and raised on a farm in North Dakota. His love of books and reading blossomed and grew from comics to sci-fi paperback books and novels, and branched into ancient cultures and their metaphysical roots. After earning a B.A. in Theatre and Drama, he studied Sacred Dance. Douglas has studied parapsychology research and is well versed in natural electromagnetics—he saw auras and ley lines as a child. He's studied and thoroughly researched all areas of metaphysics, Eastern and Western mystical and practical arts, including arts of Shamanic Journey. He taught and lectured publicly in Denver, Boston, Florida, Sedona, and London. He's currently working on his third novel in the genre of metaphysical science fiction. This gives an ample platform to share a life time of extraordinary experiences in an enjoyable way.

Carol Deanna

Carol DeAnna worked in the gaming industry for many years, but her particular interests lie in the less well-known attractions of Las Vegas, Nevada. The Wetlands Park at the end of east Tropicana Avenue, and the Springs Preserve on south Valley View Boulevard are two wonderful places to explore the beauty of the desert ecosystem, which includes the various washes that cross the Vegas Valley. When Carol began writing, she chose the genres that she loves to read: suspense, mystery and thrillers. Flamingo Wash is her first published story. She and her husband share their condo with a rescue cat named Clouseau.

John Dohanich

J M Dohanich graduated from Grand Valley State University in 1974 with a composite bachelor degree in sociol-

Contributors

ogy, arts & media. He began his writing with poetry and short stories in high school. After joining the Henderson Writers Group J M was published in the first edition of Writers Bloc. J M Dohanich worked as a staff photographer for VEGAS, an insert for the Los Angeles Herald Examiner, in the early 1980's. His photographs have also appeared in Las Vegan And Casino Internationale.

Sid Goodman

Mr. Goodman relocated from Southern California to Southern Nevada with his Southern Belle. During his career he specialized in high-tech Plastics and aerospace materials and published three major reference books, encyclopedic articles and numerous contributions to journals and governmental publications. He turned to creative writing as a major element of his retirement activities. He published a short story in the Henderson Writers' Group Anthology Writer's Bloc II and the Patchwork Path's Dad's Bow Tie. His new children's book —Grandpa's Unfatootzer—was released in May 2009.

Kathie Harrington

Kathie Harrington, M.A., CCC-SLP is a speech-language pathologist, and the mother of a child with a disability. She is an international speaker on autism and the author of two books on the topic along with numerous articles for journals, serials, and on-line continuing education units. Kathie has numerous short stories and poems in publications/anthologies: Chicken Soup Series, Chocolate for A Woman's Soul Series, and her most current short story, Shilo, a romance about adults with autism, published on-line by The Wild Rose Press. She is listed in The National Library of Poetry, and Who's Who in American Education. The Boo Cow is her self-published children's book and she blogs at www.kathiesworld.com. To Dance with Fireflies is Kathie's first novel.

Leslie Hoffman
Leslie is a writer, photographer, independent copy editor, and co-editor of PenHouseInk Press' annual literary anthologies <www.penhouseink.com>. Her poems, essays, and articles have been published in magazines, anthologies, newspapers, and on the web. Leslie's photos are sold via her line of note cards and as matted enlargements. Her "Hacienda Bridge" photo was featured on The Oprah Winfrey Show in 2002. Leslie is currently working on a book about "the draw to Las Vegas."

Carrie Ann Lahain
Carrie Ann Lahain moved to Las Vegas from New York in 2003. She has an MA in Anthropology from Rutgers. Her work has appeared in literary journals and small magazines. She has short stories forthcoming in *Italian Americana* and *Mature Living* and has recently finished drafting her third novel.

Lynn Lanier
Lynn write Science Fiction Novels. He is a member of Anthem Authors and Henderson Writers Group. His unpublished titles include *The Resurrection of Romeo*, *The Truth Kills*, and *The Magma Chronicles*. Several of his short stories have been published in anthologies. Before becoming an author, he was a chemical engineer responsible for development and manufacture of drugs and chemicals.

Linda Lou
Linda holds an M.S. in Technical Communication from Rensselaer Polytechnic Institute and has had a successful

career in technical writing and corporate training for more than 15 years. In addition to teaching workshops, she often moderates panel presentations on a variety of topics related to writing and the creative process. At press time, Linda Lou is seeking representation for her book *Shaking the Etch-a-Sketch of Life*, an autobiographical account of how she shook that Etch-a-Sketch of life and started over alone in Las Vegas after a mid-life divorce. In addition to the piece included in this anthology, she has had an excerpt from her book included in *Writer's Bloc: A Las Vegas Valley Authors' Showcase (2006)* and expects a humorous essay to be published in *Chicken Soup for the Divorced Soul in April 2008*. Contact Linda Lou at LindaHBO@aol.com.

Michael Mohony
Michael Molony has been a resident of Las Vegas since 1966 and always enjoyed the ever-changing landscape of the city. Many of the stories Michael has written are based on experiences he has had while growing up and running businesses in Las Vegas and the surrounding communities. Michael is an Internet developer with a penchant for programming and exploiting technology. Michael's blog is blog.dreamshire.com.

Michael O'Neal
Michael resides in Las Vegas, NV, where he writes for several genres, most notably horror/fantasy and science fiction. A prolific artist and playwright, he constructs visual works of horror by pen and has had several of his plays produced – Soul, Nuthouse, and Booksmart. He has been published in the anthologies Writer's Bloc III, Patchwork Path: Christmas Stocking, and most recently the horror anthology, Zombies! by Stony Meadow/Dark

Moon Publishers. His chapbook of poetry, *Enema*, is available in paperback. He is currently seeking a publisher for his second novel, *Solomon's Gate*. Contact info for all inquiries: devilsplayground@live.com.

Kevin Parsons
Kevin Parsons was born in Seattle, Washington and since 1998 has lived in Las Vegas, Nevada. He wrote and self-published *Ken Johnson and Roxi the Rocker*, a children's book available on Amazon.com, as well as numerous one act plays for Christ Church of Northgate from 1980-1996. He's also been published in *Honda Red Rider* magazine, *Racer X magazine*, Southwest Airlines' *Spirit* magazine, the *Las Vegas Review Journal* and *Cycle News* magazine. For 2 years he wrote short stories for the *MRAN* (Motorcycle Racing Association of Nevada) website. He was also a contributing writer to Seeking God First, a book of devotions. His current work, Silent Night, Holy War is the first of a trilogy series about a church surviving a terrorist attack. Kevin is a member of the Henderson Writers Group and American Christian Fiction Writers.

Debbie Prince
Currently, Debbie works as a Physical Therapist Assistant while she peruses a career in Sign Language Interpretation. She is a member in good standing of the Henderson Writer's Group and Tall Club of Las Vegas (board member social co-chair). As a resident of N. Las Vegas, she can be contacted at is debbie@talldoll.com

Nancy Sansone
Nancy's hometown is Greendale, Wisconsin. She writes suspense and short stories. Nancy's publications include a biographical profile titled *Skirts that Swept the Desert Floor*.

Contributors

Nancy received a Casino Management Degree from CCSN and holds a license for Nevada Health & Life Insurance. She is a member of the Henderson Writers Group, the Shared Word Writers Group, and the Nevada Women's History Project. Nancy has twenty years experience working in a casino in addition to raising and educating five children. Nancy's works in progress include *Calling Her Name*, a suspense novel, *Jenny*, a biographic short story, and *The Last Laugh*, a short story. Nancy enjoys genealogy, travel, and dining out.

Glory Wade
Glory Wade writes short stories in various genres. Her published credentials include a chapter in the 5th edition of the Professional Meeting Management textbook, dog training and newsletter articles, and copy for a jewelry publication. She is completing her first novel, *Ashes to Diamonds, Dust to Dust*.

W. Darrah Whitaker
W. Darrah Whitaker was born and raised in Birmingham, Alabama. He is a graduate of the University of Virginia and holds two Masters degress (MA/MBA) from the University of Texas. He has tried his hand at screenwriting, completing four screenplays, one of which was produced. Recently, he moved from the Los Angeles area and currently resides in Henderson, Nevada where he manages his aviation software company. He spends the balance of his time with his two children, running, and working on the completion of his first novel.

Roger Storkamp
Roger Storkamp sought refuge in Las Vegas after thirty-five years of teaching high school, to release the characters who

invaded his psyche while growing up in rural Minnesota. He has since written three literary novels set in Bovine, Minnesota, a town without a zip code. He holds a Master of Arts degree from the University of Wisconsin and did post graduate work at Pepperdine University, California, Nova University, Florida, Fordham University, New York, and Texas and Minnesota State Universities. He taught education courses at United States International University in San Diego. He earned a Doctor of Arts degree from East Coast University in Florida.

Jo A. Wilkins

Jo is the founder and president of the Henderson Writers' Group. Her avid reading of Science Fiction (Isaac Asimov and C.J Cherryh are among her favorite authors) brought her to writing Science Fiction under the name of J.A. Wilkins. She also incorporates what she reads in science journals into her writing. Jo has won awards as a poet, and is co-author of the *Tyranny* series, which currently includes *Tyranny's Outpost*, *Tyranny's Prisoner*, and *Tyranny's Alliance* (there are 2 more books planned for the series). In addition to the *Tyranny* series, she is developing a murder mystery. Jo is a co-founder of Mystic Publishers, a company steeped in the philosophy of customer satisfaction.

Brian Yates

Brian T. Yates is a member of the Henderson Writers' Group and the author of Yalu and the Puppy Room, a children's book, due out in hard cover on April 1, 2010. This is a first in a series of books about a Golden Retriever looking for a forever home. Brian is also the author of Joey's War, a novel set in 1997 New York City where an up and coming La Cosa Nostra associate rises through the ranks to become the undisputed boss of New York City.